THE AUTOBIOGRAPHY OF MRS. OLIPHANT

From a drawing made in 1895 by Janet Mary Oliphant.

Walker & Boutall, ph. sc.

THE AUTOBIOGRAPHY OF
MRS. OLIPHANT

Arranged and Edited by

MRS. HARRY COGHILL

With a new Foreword by

LAURIE LANGBAUER

THE UNIVERSITY OF CHICAGO PRESS

Chicago & London

The University of Chicago Press, Chicago 60637
The University of Chicago Press, Ltd., London

© *1988 by The University of Chicago*
All rights reserved. Published 1899.
University of Chicago Press edition 1988
Printed in the United States of America

97 96 95 94 93 92 91 90 89 88   5 4 3 2 1

Library of Congress Cataloging in Publication Data

Oliphant, Mrs. (Margaret), 1828–1897.
   [Autobiography and letters of Mrs. M.O.W. Oliphant]
   The autobiography of Mrs. Oliphant / arranged and edited by Mrs.
Harry Coghill ; with a new foreword by Laurie Langbauer. —
University of Chicago Press ed.
      p.   cm.
   Partial reprint. Originally published: The autobiography and
letters of Mrs. M.O.W. Oliphant. New York : Dodd, Mead,
1899. Letters omitted.
   Bibliography: p.
   1. Oliphant, Mrs. (Margaret), 1828–1897—Biography.   2. Oliphant,
Mrs. (Margaret), 1828–1897—Correspondence.   3. Novelists,
Scottish—19th century—Correspondence.   4. Novelists,
Scottish—19th century—Biography.   I. Coghill, Harry, Mrs.,
d. 1907.   II. Title.
PR5114.A3   1988
823'.8—dc19
[B]   87–33280
ISBN 0-226-62651-2 (pbk.)   CIP

FOREWORD

An Ordinary Woman

"There is nothing so costly as bargains," Margaret Oliphant once wrote to a friend, referring to the seductions of old lace, but the danger in cheapening costly wonders provides an implicit analogy (as the sharp and self-ironic Oliphant well knew) with her own reception—or of all the legend of it that remains to us: the cautionary tale of a gifted writer who sold herself cheap, wasting her talents through her very industry. For although Oliphant was in her time well-known and popular—over the course of her life, which neatly spans the Victorian era, she wrote almost one hundred novels, several hundred periodical articles, numerous short stories, histories, and biographies—now not yet a century after her death most of this work has disappeared. Too prolific, it appears, by making herself a household name she became a commonplace (and hence an ultimately and appropriately forgotten) one. References to her works have customarily become simply an account of their quantity like the one above, a bill of lading turning her production into so much merchandise, too much, so that (such accounts imply) it is no surprise that they became a drug on the literary marketplace.

Perhaps the work that has best endured, standing removed from such general depreciation, has been her *Autobiography* (1899). It has certainly never been ranked as a classic statement of the Victorian self-questioning spirit, never been canonized as a testament to what she herself calls "a fashion of self-explanation which belongs to the time," in the way that Newman's *Apologia,* Mill's *Autobiography,* or Ruskin's *Praeterita* (published respectively about thirty, twenty five, and ten years before Oliphant's work) have been. Yet references to her *Autobiography* suggest that—as a woman's life story—it continues to be attractive although it has never been institutionalized, and perhaps precisely because the experiences it recounts are in direct opposition to the assumptions behind the literary institution. (References to it appear in our own time in Elaine Showalter's *A Literature of Their Own,* for example.) But rather than creating an underground for the rest of her work and partially remedying Oliphant's obscurity these may, on the contrary, contribute to that obscurity by contributing to the legend that explains and enforces it.[1]

Despite what may actually be a willed indifference to her works owing to the demands of gender ideologies, Oliphant's *Autobiography* has continued to receive attention. This is because, in one way, it is a classic example of its genre: the poignant self-division that characterizes it, as current critical studies of the form suggest, points beyond its author's particular experience to the contradictions within constructions of identity and meaning.[2] And Oliphant, as a reader and reviewer of autobiography— she refers in her own to Trollope's and Symonds's, for instance—was sensitive to its formal complexities as well as to the impulses motivating them. But what is distinctive about such contradiction in Oliphant's work is not that it exists, but where she locates it. Her characteristic attitude—feeling "half sorry for myself and half ashamed of myself," as she calls it—bespeaks a division of a peculiar kind. Although Oliphant records in these pages that she has never been taken at her proper value as a writer, she at the same time claims the fault as entirely her own. Her autobiography is both a lament and apology—a lament that she has been sold too cheap and an apology for having done the cheapening herself.[3]

The effect of such claims is important, for it suggests that the *Autobiography* may share, if not assume to itself, an attitude toward women that is very much a part of the social and literary dogma which insists that women (and women writers) are not simply different, but inferior. It suggests that readers return to the *Autobiography*'s pages now and then not to rectify Oliphant's obscurity, but to validate it and be reassured about it. If we wished to make this work conform in another way as a classic Victorian autobiography, we could say that it too (despite its wry and unpretentious wit) records the utterance of a sage. But what Oliphant utters as sage is a self-fulfilling prophecy of her own failure. The Oliphant legend is, in a sense, the self-creation of Margaret Oliphant, the self she creates in her autobiography. Her reputation as a hack, whose industry is an equivocal virtue which blights a promise deserving better economy, is established by her own hand in this work, just as Trollope's autobiography is blamed for obscuring his merits after his death. Critics like the Colbys, who confirm Oliphant as a minor talent, are simply repeating the gesture of her text.[4] And this is a gesture of which the text is well aware. Several times within it, Oliphant's autobiographical narrator predicts that her reception depends on her self-presentation: "I feel that my carelessness of asserting my claim is very much against me with everybody," she tells us even as she invents the legend of that carelessness. Just who, then, is willing the indifference that results in Oliphant's current oblivion? What does Oliphant gain, and what does she lose, in making it her own responsibility?

Anyone who reads the *Autobiography* learns that taking (too much) responsibility is, as Oliphant tells us, both her

strength and her weakness. Pretending to such responsibility in this case, notwithstanding its masochism, may
represent as it does throughout Oliphant's life the only
claim to control and power available to (writing) women.
Oliphant's self-criticism grants her at least the illusion of
autonomy: it anticipates the reception awaiting a woman
attempting to write, and especially to write a self in an
autobiography. Her attitude toward herself denies her
value because value and even selfhood are denied women
as their culture constructs them anyway. Acceding to
such constraints might seem to provide its own consola-
tions, even its own (illusory) access to the power system
that rejects and regulates her. Certainly the picture of
Oliphant in painful collusion with the system comes
across in her autobiography, and letters as her editor and
niece, Annie Coghill, bowdlerized them. One of the few
references to the woman question that Coghill includes—
part of a letter referring to Mill's "mad notion of the
franchise for women"—describes Oliphant's disregard of
self-respect when it came to placing her sons, for example. Her begging in their behalf for an introduction to
the old boy's network that ignored and excluded her is
made to seem part of a characteristic posture of selling
out. But the tenor of the *Autobiography* itself seems to
allow such editorial choices. The excuse with which
Oliphant justifies but also establishes her minor status,
that the faults of her writing were necessary and natural
to her duties as a mother, seizes on that role for women
most sanctioned by culture. In its embrace of such values, Oliphant's autobiography can seem profoundly
conservative. It reverses with a vengeance the pattern of
resistance to their roles that a critic such as Nancy K.
Miller has charted in the autobiographies of those women
writers who renounce or marginalize maternity, insisting
that they are mothers by accident, but writers by design.[5]
    Yet that these other writers in some way conceive their
autobiographies in terms of conception makes Oliphant's

insistence on maternity seem other than just a sell-out; it can seem also the strategy of the (m)other, making use of the roles, images, and values available to her, but radically rewriting them in her own way to record her dissatisfaction and revolt. Oliphant's most recent biographer points out that, despite the skewing of the *Autobiography*, if we look at her work as a whole we get a picture of a woman extremely sympathetic and committed to women's struggles.[6] And such conservatism is not even really to be found in Oliphant's *Autobiography*, but only the illusion of it, just as her attempt in those pages to make maternity and authorship mutually exclusive fails to convince us in the face of other evidence to the contrary. She tells a friend "alas! 'thae muving things ca'ed weans'" have forced her to be careless of her reputation (the cry might almost be the epigraph to the *Autobiography*), and most of the *Autobiography* claims that her identity as a mother quite properly if still painfully undermines her identity as a writer. But she also tells us almost on the first page that this is a false opposition: "the big fact that it was necessary for me to work for my children," she admits, only provides a smokescreen, "a way of eluding the question which I have neither time nor wish to enter into"—the question of her identity and value as a writer.

Her emphasis on motherhood, in fact, might not really elude the issue of writing at all, but rather provide another way to imagine and work through the problems of creation. Barbara Johnson has recently argued that women's writing, autobiography, and motherhood are profoundly interrelated, all reflecting the peculiar problems of representation and identity exposed in the cultural construction of women. Johnson calls "the desire for resemblance, the desire to create a being like oneself" the "autobiographical desire par excellence";[7] for Oliphant, the experience of motherhood especially involves the problem of resemblance and separation. What her experience teaches is the impossibility of marking out an autonomous identity, a name (and the meaning of names especially intrigues Oliphant throughout her autobiography), the impossibility of creating one being that resembles herself without killing others off. In a sense, she feels she survives as Margaret because her mother Margaret (who seems figuratively to give way when her daughter becomes a mother herself) and her daughter Margaret do not. We see Oliphant's sense of the price of her own self-creation in the guilt she feels at her mother's death (and her daughter's? How else to explain the gnawing and persistent insinuation throughout the *Autobiography* that rather than her inspiration her children are the deadweights that sink her writing?).

Yet the guilt here does not entirely hide that the fantasy of killing others accords the self wrestling with the problems of creation an illusion of freedom and almost total power—the power not just to create but also to destroy subjects. And we get the impression from reading this autobiography, watching her provide for and manage an extended family totally dependent on her, that Oliphant embraced her motherhood because it was an arena in which she felt complete control. Although she makes a cult of her sons, the other women in her family always seem most important and attractive to Oliphant, because they share her powers as a manager. But if she respects the Oliphant women because of the great capabilities they share as a family trait, such common strengths are also most threatening to her autonomy. Moreover, as Oliphant writes in an essay, "The Grievances of Women," just as the name and abilities connect the women in her family, (too closely) identifying them with each other, another inheritance passes from mother to daughter: a sense of injustice that women must necessarily feel for the treatment they receive in the world of men.[8] By ascribing to herself the (partly wishful) ability to destroy the very line of inheritance on which such injustice operates, Oliphant seems to stand alone and outside it, freeing herself from its constraints. Translating the problems of writing into the problems of motherhood allows her a way imaginatively to respond to and redress her own sense of injustice, by granting her a devastating power.

Yet the effectiveness, if not also the subversiveness, of such a strategy is ultimately in question, for the one ultimately devastated, of course, is Oliphant herself. She must kill off her mother and daughter, especially, in order to write, yet both, as *Margarets*, are figuratively but absolutely part of herself. No matter then that in her obsessive self-criticism she asks over and over, "am I at fault?" not just about the deaths of these self-evident alter-egos, but of her sons too. No matter that this self-critical voice may hide the inevitable desire of the oppressed for justice, and even for its own megalomaniacal revenge. Whatever her attitude, Oliphant's life story can finally only record the sheer disposability, the planned obsolescence, of the self in the indifferent throw-away economy within which it circulates. The agonizing ending of Oliphant's autobiography ("And now here I am all alone. I cannot write anymore") suggests that its ultimate effect—literally writing her out of existence as far as posterity is concerned—is only the logical conclusion of the impulses forming it. It is the woman writer's last accession, both accepted and resisted, to the system of power authorizing her.

But the language in which Oliphant describes this inevitability gives us a way to read it that exposes the workings of the system even if it does not arrest them. For in characterizing herself as, above all, a mother, Oliphant is also reiterating and foregrounding her ordinariness. Her "prosaic little narrative, all about the facts of a life so simple," demonstrates, she tells us, that a mother's story, especially compared to the stories of men, can only be drab. Yet, given Oliphant's self-division, the reason for her insistence on the drab seems to be more than what Patricia Spacks suggests about other women autobiographers: that "they declare the self's reality and significance by heightening its experience. To turn happenings into stories, to tell somebody, makes the trivial seem to matter."[9] By insisting that the demands of motherhood—woman's most ordinary role—have kept her a commonplace writer, Oliphant establishes an insistent metaphor of the debased, humdrum, and commonplace, one that runs throughout the *Autobiography*. The metaphor is so pervasive that it suggests more than just a bitter (because rather extraordinary) woman trying to come to terms with a common world that can only judge her by its ordinary measure. Oliphant's emphasis does not so much make the ordinary important as embrace its unimportance, asking us to come to terms with it.

By forcing the commonplace on us, as much as by forcing herself to it, Oliphant makes us unable to accept it without question as simply the determining category of her life's story, the bottom line sufficient in itself in explaining her own markdown. Rather, this emphasis asks us to question the ordinary as a category, to question what an appeal to it might mean. As Oliphant tells us, nothing is so costly as bargains—that is, costly to us too in our unthinking assumption of how such discounts work. An appeal to the ordinary, the discounting of a writer like Oliphant because she is somehow common—too general, accustomed, widespread, but also inferior, low, cheap—comes only at a price. Oliphant's oblivion is expensive not just because it makes her experience as unavailable to us, say, as Mary Wollstonecraft's was to her (when she was preparing her own literary history, she had to beg Blackwood to hunt up the long unpublished *Vindication of the Rights of Woman*). And it is unavailable perhaps for the same reason: because it suggests possibilities for or at least problems of women that expose the assumptions constraining them. But, more specifically, ignoring Oliphant because we tell ourselves that she is a commonplace writer helps maintain the power of the ordinary, for constraint is enacted precisely at that level. Because we accept that the ordinary is by definition unimportant, we blind ourselves to its real effects, to the unremarkable but prohibitive costs of that category— to the power of our oblivion to its workings, and the oblivions enforced in its name.

Laurie Langbauer

NOTES

1. Elaine Showalter, *A Literature of Their Own: British Women Novelists from Brontë to Lessing* (Princeton, NJ: Princeton University Press, 1977); for her recounting of the accepted interpretation of Oliphant's life and influence, see, e.g.,
"Mrs. Oliphant, for example, fought a never-ending battle against bankruptcy. The sole support of her own children, and her nephews as well, she lived in perpetual bondage to a string of publishers, selling ideas for books she had not begun to write, and writing books she never cared for, simply to stay ahead. The British Museum has volumes of her letters to publishers, begging for an advance, or referring to a series of travel books, biographies, or textbooks that she was churning out. To Virginia Woolf, these circumstances explain the poverty of her art: 'Mrs Oliphant sold her brain, her very admirable brain, prostituted her culture and enslaved her intellectual liberty in order that she might earn her living and educate her children'" (p. 47).

2. For a classic statement on the (de)construction of the autobiographical form, see Paul de Man, "Autobiography as De-facement," *MLN* 94 (1979): 919–30.

3. For a reading that accounts for the divisions of Oliphant's text differently, in terms of the change in her projected audience, see. Linda H. Peterson, "Audience and the Autobiographer's Art: An Approach to the *Autobiography* of Mrs. M. O. W. Oliphant," in *Approaches to Victorian Autobiography*, ed. George P. Landow (Athens, OH: Ohio University Press, 1979), 158–74.

4. Vineta and Robert Colby, *The Equivocal Virtue: Mrs. Oliphant and the Victorian Literary Market Place* (New York: Archon Books, 1966).

5. Nancy K. Miller, "Women's Autobiography in France: For a Dialectics of Identification," in *Women and Language in Literature and Society*, ed. Sally McConnell-Ginet, Ruth Borker, and Nelly Furman (New York: Praeger Publishers, 1980), 258–73. Miller argues that

"the autobiographies of these women . . . are a defense and illustration, at once a treatise on overcoming received notions of femininity,
and a poetics calling for another, freer test" (263).

6. Merryn Williams, *Margaret Oliphant: A Critical Biography* (New
York: St. Martin's Press, 1986), especially 106–12.

7. Barbara Johnson, "My Monster/My Self," in her *A World of
Difference* (Baltimore: Johns Hopkins University Press, 1987), 146.

8. Published in *Fraser's Magazine,* May 1880. I am indebted to
Williams's biography for bringing this essay to my attention.

9. Patricia Meyer Spacks, *Imagining a Self: Autobiography and
Novel in Eighteenth-Century England* (Cambridge: Harvard University Press, 1976), 78.

CONTENTS.

III.

IV.

PREFACE.

In some of the last words she ever wrote, Mrs Oliphant described herself as "a writer very little given to explanations or to any personal appearance"; and probably of no writer that ever lived was this so absolutely true a description. Her work, enormous in volume and multifarious in kind, was given to the public; her life was for her children first, and after them for the small circle of loving and intimate friends who closely surrounded her. Of these, many, in the last darkening years of her life, had passed away, and with one small exception it is in these years only that we find in her writings any personal revelations, intentional or unintentional. They were very rarely intentional, and when they were, it was of deliberate purpose and for a fixed reason, as in two recent papers in 'Blackwood'—" The Thoughts of a Believer" and "The Verdict of Old Age." The last and most touching instance is in the only preface which she ever attached to a novel—the few pages called "On the Ebb Tide," prefacing 'The Ways of Life.'

When she wrote those pages, worn out with bodily and mental suffering, she thought she felt in herself the beginnings of failure. As a matter of fact, she had never written more brilliantly than at times during the concluding year of her life; but she had never since the

death of her last child been conscious of that happy
mastery of her work which had supplied many of the
pleasantest hours of the past. " I am behind the fashion,"
she said herself; " I have no longer the place or the value
I had." She felt certain that the difficulty of producing
good work must increase for her (as, indeed, at sixty-
nine it well might), and she greatly longed to be released
from her service and allowed to join those who had gone
before her. But until within the last few months she
had very little hope of escape. When first those who
loved her were anxious, alarmed by her pallor, her inability to take food, and what they knew of her nights
of sleepless sorrow, she used to smile and say, " Don't
be afraid; there never is anything the matter with me."
Her health had almost always been perfect, withstanding
every kind of fatigue and sorrow, and she could not think
that it would fail her. But when, only about ten days
before the end, it became certain that she was mortally
ill, she said, as she had imagined Mr Sandford saying,
" God is very good; He gives me everything."

In this quiet confidence that everything had been so
perfectly arranged for her, with her mind clear, even a
little flicker of fun in her eyes at times, always a tender
smile and word for those she loved, a great writer passed
away from us, leaving a blank that there is certainly no
one capable of filling. There have been, perhaps there
are (and she herself would have been the first to say it
with full belief), greater novelists, but who has ever
achieved the same variety of literary work with anything like the same level of excellence? A great deal
of her very best remains at present anonymous — bio-
graphical and critical papers, and others dealing with
an extraordinary variety of subjects. But merely to
divide her books into classes gives some little idea of
the range of her powers. Her novels, long and short,

can hardly number much less than a hundred, but these for a long time back were by no means her works of predilection; and in the three last sad years all fiction had been heavy labour to her. Next in importance come her biographies — Edward Irving, Count de Montalembert, Principal Tulloch, Laurence Oliphant, and a number of smaller ones, some involving great labour and research; while her last work of this class, two volumes of the 'History of the House of Blackwood,' occupied two years of her life. Then there are the brilliant papers on the reign of George II., collected some years ago, and those on the reign of Queen Anne; the laborious, but not entirely successful, 'Literary History of England,' and 'A Child's History of Scotland.' 'The Makers of Florence' began a fresh series in 1876; it was followed at intervals by 'The Makers of Venice,' 'Rome,' and 'Jerusalem,' each of these books involving immense labour, and all, except 'Rome,' having its materials carefully collected on the spot. The topography of Rome she knew well; every aspect of it had been engraved on her memory with the pencil of sorrow. Finally, there remains one of the most wonderful set of writings in our language—that which began very simply and sweetly with 'A Little Pilgrim,' and went on through various 'Stories of the Seen and the Unseen,' reaching a strange poetic power and beauty in 'A Beleaguered City,' and finding, to those who were near enough to her life to guess the thoughts with which it was written, a most fitting end in 'The Land of Suspense.' Thus she had laboured in almost every field of literature, winning every kind of success, and never, in all the fifty years (except, perhaps, for one moment in the early days of her widowhood), making a real failure. One day in the last week of her life she said, " Many times I have come to a corner which I could see no way round, but each time

a way has been found for me." The way was often
found by the strengthening of her own indomitable
courage, which, as long as her children were left to her,
never seemed to flag,—it was the courage of perfect love.
But it is certain that if she had had no moral qualities
except courage, she could not have toiled on as she did:
a saving sense of humour, a great capacity to enjoy what
was really comic and everything that was beautiful, made
life easier to her, and "the great joy of doing kindnesses"
was one never absent from her. So that whatever suffering might be lying in wait to seize upon her solitary
hours, there was almost always a pleasant welcome and
talk of the very best to be found in her modest drawing-
room. If the visitors were congenial, her charm of
manner awoke, her simple fitness of speech clothed
every subject with life and grace, her beautiful eyes
shone (they never sparkled), and the spell of her exquisite womanliness made a charmed circle round her.
She was never a beautiful woman at any time of her
life, though for many years she was a very pretty one,
but she had, as a family inheritance, lovely hands, which
were constantly busy, in what she called her idle time,
with some dainty sewing or knitting; she had those
wonderful eyes which kept their beauty to the last
minute of her life; and she had a most exquisite dainti-
ness in all her ways and in the very atmosphere about
her which was "pure womanly."

It was just at the moment when all England kept
festival for the Queen's second Jubilee—in the last half
of June 1897—that Mrs Oliphant lay dying in a sunny
little house at Wimbledon. Happily free from acute
pain, she had passed into a serene region of perfect
peace, out of which she spoke to us who were about
her with all her old brightness, giving such information
and directions as she thought might be useful *after*.

And one distinct injunction she laid upon us—no biography of her was to be written.

Many years ago she had begun in a time of great trial and loneliness to write down scraps more or less autobiographical, and later had added more cheerful pictures of her early life. Later still, to please her last surviving child, she continued this memoir, bringing it up to the time when her two sons went to Oxford. She must, it would seem, have intended to add to it some record of the remaining twenty years of her life, and possibly in her last hours she forgot how great a gap was left. At any rate she bade us deal with this autobiography as we thought best, believing that it would serve for all that was necessary.

But when those to whom she had intrusted it came to examine the manuscript, a great disappointment befell them. It had no beginning; scraps had been written at long intervals and by no means consecutively. The first entry in her book was written in 1860, and mentions, rather than records, the struggles of her early widowhood. The second, in 1864, is the outpouring of her grief for the loss of her one daughter, her little Maggie, suddenly snatched from her in Rome. After this is the long gap of twenty-one years, till the time when in her bright house at Windsor with both her sons still left to her, and her two adopted daughters about her, she was moved to write down a more connected and less sad record. But even then the thread is snapped two or three times before it finally breaks off after the death of both her sons, and it may be that the needful fitting together has not been quite smoothly done after all.

So far, however, there is a narrative in her own writing. After 1892 there is nothing, and it seemed impossible to allow the late years of her life — full of work, full of varying scenes and interests—to remain altogether un-

recorded. The best thing that could be done, therefore,
was to supplement her manuscript with letters, and to
connect these with the slightest possible thread of story,
thus endeavouring to obey her wishes and yet gratify
the many readers who have for so long a stretch of years
regarded her as a friend.

Here, however, another and most unexpected difficulty
occurred. Three or four of her most intimate friends
—two especially to whom she was in the habit of writing
full and interesting letters—have died within the last
few years, and the whole correspondences which would
have been so valuable have been destroyed. One series
of letters, beginning in 1865 and ending only with her
death, is too intimate to furnish much of general interest,
though a few selections from it are given; and several
friends have added each two or three letters to the
collection. The largest portion of the correspondence
now printed belongs to the Blackwood family. Her
faithful and highly valued friend, the late Mr John
Blackwood, his sister the late Miss Blackwood, and Mr
William Blackwood, the present Editor of ' Maga,' were
all recipients of letters which are very characteristic and
very interesting, and give almost a connected history of
Mrs Oliphant's literary work. Some others come from Mr
Craik (Macmillan & Co.), and some from other business
correspondents. A few letters to her sons have been
added, and in all cases it has seemed advisable to furnish
now and then a letter written *to* her to explain those
written *by* her.

Very little more than this has been attempted. Only
when the end must be chronicled another hand takes
up the pen she has laid down and sorrowfully records
the close of a life—not faultless, indeed, but noble, loving,
and womanly in the highest sense, and of a literary
career full of sound, skilful, and serviceable labours.

Let me end this short preface with an extract from a letter addressed to Mr Blackwood in 1876, and expressing her feeling with regard to one from Mr Kinglake:—

"How very good of Mr Kinglake to interest himself about the poor little reputation which, alas! 'thae muving things ca'ed weans' have forced me to be so careless of. . . . I think, though, if ever the time comes that I can lie on my oars, after the boys are out in the world, or when the time comes which there is no doubt about, when I shall be out of the world, that I will get a little credit—but not much now, there is so much of me!"

A. L. C.

March 1899.

THE AUTOBIOGRAPHY OF MRS. OLIPHANT

Walker & Boutall, ph sc

Windsor 1874.

M.O.W.O.   O.F.O.

F.R.O.   F.W.

AUTOBIOGRAPHY.

———◆———

I.

Windsor, 1st February 1885.[1]

TWENTY-ONE years have passed since I wrote what is on the opposite page.[2] I have just been reading it all with tears ; sorry, very sorry for that poor soul who has lived through so much since. Twenty-one years is a little lifetime. It is curious to think that I was not very young, nearly thirty-six, at that time, and that I am not very old, nearly fifty-seven, now. Life, though it is short, is very long, and contains so much. And one does not, to one's consciousness, change as one's outward appearance and capabilities do. Doesn't Mrs Somerville say that, so far from feeling old, she was not always quite certain (up in the seventies) whether she was quite grown up! I entirely understand the feeling, though I have had enough, one would think, to make one feel old. Since the time when that most unexpected, most terrible blow overtook me in Rome — where her father had died four years before — I have had trials which, I say it with

---

[1] It has been thought better to print the earlier portion, or such of it as might interest general readers, after this part of Mrs. Oliphant's journal, so as to preserve the sequence of the narrative. — Ed.

[2] See Preface, p. ix. — Ed.

full knowledge of all the ways of mental suffering, have been harder than sorrow. I have lived a laborious life, incessant work, incessant anxiety — and yet so strange, so capricious is this human being, that I would not say I have had an unhappy life. I have said this to one or two friends who know faintly without details what I have had to go through, and astonished them. Sometimes I am miserable — always there is in me the sense that I may have active cause to be so at any moment — always the gnawing pangs of anxiety, and deep, deep dissatisfaction beyond words, and the sense of helplessness, which of itself is despair. And yet there are times when my heart jumps up in the old unreasonable way, and I am, — yes, happy — though the word seems so inappropriate — without any cause for it, with so many causes the other way. I wonder whether this is want of feeling, or mere temperament and elasticity, or if it is a special compensation — " Werena my heart licht I wad dee " — Grizel Hume must have had the same.

I have been tempted to begin writing by George Eliot's life — with that curious kind of self-compassion which one cannot get clear of. I wonder if I am a little envious of her? I always avoid considering formally what my own mind is worth. I have never had any theory on the subject. I have written because it gave me pleasure, because it came natural to me, because it was like talking or breathing, besides the big fact that it was necessary for me to work for my children. That, however, was not the first motive, so that when I laugh inquiries off and say that it is my trade, I do it only by way of eluding the question which I have neither time nor wish to enter into. Anthony Trollope's talk about the characters in his books astonished me beyond measure, and I am totally incapable of talking about anything I have ever done in that way. As he was a thoroughly sensible genuine man, I suppose he was quite sincere in what he says of them, — or was it that he was driven into a fashion of self-explanation which belongs to the time, and which I am following now though in another way? I feel that my carelessness of asserting my claim is very much against me with everybody. It is so natural to think that if the workman himself is indifferent about his work, there can't be much in it that is worth thinking about. I am not indifferent, yet I should rather like to forget it all, to wipe out all the books, to silence those compliments about my industry, &c., which I always turn off with a laugh. I suppose this is really pride, with a mixture of Scotch shyness, and a good deal of that uncomprehended, unexplainable feeling which made Mrs Carlyle reply with a jibe, which meant only a whimsical impulse to take the side of opposition, and the strong Scotch sense of the absurdity of a chorus of praise, but which looks so often like detraction and bitterness, and has now definitely been accepted as such by the public in general. I don't find words to express it adequately, but I feel it strenuously in my own case. When people comment upon the number of books I have written, and I say that I am so far from being proud of that fact that I should like at least half of them forgotten, they stare — and yet it is quite true; and even here I could no more go solemnly into them, and tell why I had done this or that, than I could fly. They are my work, which I like in the doing, which is my natural way of occupying myself, though they are never so good as I meant them to be. And when I have said that, I have said all that is in me to say.

I don't quite know why I should put this all down. I suppose because George Eliot's life has, as I said above, stirred me up to an involuntary confession. How I have been handicapped in life! Should I have done better if I had been kept, like her, in a mental greenhouse and taken care of? This is one of the things it is perfectly impossible to tell. In all likelihood our minds and our circumstances are so arranged that, after all, the possible way is the way that is best; yet it is a little hard sometimes not to feel with Browning's Andrea, that the men who have no wives, who have given themselves up to their art, have had an almost unfair advantage over us who have been given perhaps more than one Lucrezia to take care of. And to feel with him that perhaps in the after-life four square walls in the New Jerusalem may be given for another trial! I used to be intensely impressed in the Laurence Oliphants with that curious freedom from human ties which I have never known; and that they felt it possible to make up their minds to do what was best, without any sort of *arrière pensée*, without having to consider whether they could or not. Curious freedom! I have never known what it was. I have always had to think of other people, and to plan everything — for my own pleasure, it is true, very often, but always in subjection to the neccessity which bound me to them. On the whole, I have had a great deal of my own way, and have insisted upon getting what I wished, but only at the cost of infinite labour, and of carrying a whole little world with me whenever I moved. I have not been able to rest, to please myself, to take the pleasures that have come in my way, but have always been forced to go on without a pause. When my poor brother's family fell upon my hands, and especially when there was question of Frank's education, I remember that I said to myself, having then perhaps a little stirring of ambition, that I must make up my mind to think no more of that, and that to bring up the boys for the service of God was better than to write a fine novel, supposing even that it was in me to do so. Alas! the work has been done; the education is over; my good Frank, my steady, good boy, is dead. It seemed rather a fine thing to make that resolution (though in reality I had no choice); but now I think that if I had taken the other way, which seemed the less noble, it might have been better for all of us. I might have done better work. I should in all probability have earned nearly as much for half the production had I done less; and I might have had the satisfaction of knowing that there was something laid up for them and for my old age; while they might have learned habits of work which now seem beyond recall. Who can tell? I did with much labour what I thought the best, and there is only a *might have been* on the other side.

In this my resolution which I did make, I was, after all, only following my instincts, it being in reality easier to me to keep on with a flowing sail, to keep my household and make a number of people comfortable, at the cost of incessant work, and an occasional great crisis of anxiety, than to live the self-restrained life which the greater artist imposes upon himself.

What casuists we are on our own behalf! — this is altogether self-defence. And I know I am giving myself the air of being *au fond* a finer sort of character than the others. I may as well take the little satisfaction to myself, for nobody will give it to me. No one even will mention me in the same breath with George Eliot. And that is just. It is a little justification to myself to think how much better off she was, — no trouble in all her life as far as appears, but the natural one of her father's death — and perhaps coolnesses with her brothers and sisters, though that is not said. And though her marriage is not one that most of us would have ventured on, still it seems to have secured her a worshipper unrivalled. I think she must have been a dull woman with a great genius distinct from herself, something like the gift of the old prophets, which they sometimes exercised with only a dim sort of perception what it meant. But this is a thing to be said only with bated breath, and perhaps further thought on the subject may change even my mind. She took herself with tremendous seriousness, that is evident, and was always on duty, never relaxing, her letters ponderous beyond description — and those to the Bray party giving one the idea of a mutual improvement society for the exchange of essays.

Let me be done with this — I wonder if I will ever have time to put a few autobiographical bits down before I die. I am in very little danger of having my life written, and that is all the better in this point of view — for what could be said of me? George Eliot and George Sand make me half inclined to cry over my poor little unappreciated self — " Many love me (*i.e.*, in a sort of way), but by none am I enough beloved." These two bigger women did things which I have never felt the least temptation to do — but how very much more enjoyment they seem to have got out of their life, how much more praise and homage and honour! I would not buy their fame with these disadvantages, but I do feel very small, very obscure, beside them, rather a failure all round, never securing any strong affection, and throughout my life, though I have had all the usual experiences of woman, never impressing anybody, — what a droll little complaint! — why should I? I acknowledge frankly that there is nothing in me — a fat, little, commonplace woman, rather tongue-tied — to impress any one; and yet there is a sort of whimsical injury in it which makes me sorry for myself.

Feb. 8th.

Here, then, for a little try at the autobiography. I ought to be doing some work, getting on a little in advance for to-morrow, which gives a special zest to doing nothing:[1] to doing what has no need to be done — and Sunday evenings have always been a time to *fantasticare*, to do what one pleased ; and I have dropped out of the letter I used to do on these occasions, having — which, by the way, is a little sad when one comes to think of it — no one to write to, of anything that is beneath the surface. Curious! I had scarcely realised it before. Now for a beginning.

I remember nothing of Wallyford, where I was born, but opened my eyes to life, so far as I remember, in the village of Lasswade, where we lived in a little house, I think, on the road to Dalkeith. I recollect the wintry road ending to my consciousness in a slight ascent with

---

[1] This is exactly what Sir Walter says in his Diary, only published in 1890, so I was like him in this without knowing it.

big ash-trees forming a sort of arch; underneath which I fancy was a toll-bar, the way into the world appropriately barred by that turnpike. But no, that was not the way into the world; for the world was Edinburgh, the coach for which, I am almost sure, went the other way through the village and over the bridge to the left hand, starting from somewhere close to Mr Todd the baker's shop, of which I have a faint and kind recollection. It was by that way that Frank came home on Saturday nights to spend Sunday at home, walking out from Edinburgh (about six miles) to walk in again on Monday in the dark winter mornings. I recollect nothing about the summer mornings when he set out on that walk, but remember vividly like a picture the Monday mornings in winter; the fire burning cheerfully and candles on the breakfast-table, all dark but with a subtle sense of morning, though it seemed a kind of dissipation to be up so long before the day. I can see myself, a small creature seated on a stool by the fire, toasting a cake of dough which was brought for me by the baker with the prematurely early rolls, which were for Frank. (This dough was the special feature of the morning to me, and I suppose I had it only on these occasions.) And my mother, who never seemed to sit down in the strange, little, warm, bright picture, but to hover about the table pouring out tea, supplying everything he wanted to her boy (how proud, how fond of him! — her eyes liquid and bright with love as she hovered about); and Frank, the dearest of companions so long — then long separated, almost alien-ated, brought back again at the end to my care. How bright he was then, how good always to me, how fond of his little sister! — impatient by moments, good always. And he was a kind of god to me — *my* Frank, as I always called him. I remember once weeping bitterly over a man singing in the street, a buttoned-up, shabby-genteel man, whom, on being questioned why I cried, I ac-knowledged I thought like my Frank. That was when he was absent, and my mother's anxiety reflected in a

child's mind went, I suppose, the length of fancying that
Frank too might have to sing in the street. (He would
have come off very badly in that case, for he did not
know one tune from another, much less could he sing a
note!) How well I recollect the appearance of the man
in his close-buttoned black coat, with his dismal song,
and the acute anguish of the thought that Frank might
have come to that for anything I knew. Frank, however, never gave very much anxiety; it was Willie, poor
Willie, who was our sore and constant trouble — Willie,
who lives still in Rome, as he has done for the last two-
or three-and-twenty years — nearly a quarter of a century
— among strangers who are kind to him, wanting nothing, I hope, yet also having outlived everything. I
shrank from going to see him when I was in Italy, which
was wrong; but how can I return to Rome, and how
could he have come to me? — poor Willie! the hand-
somest, brightest of us all, with eyes that ran over with
fun and laughter — and the hair which we used to say he
had to poll, like Absalom, so many times a-year. Alas!

What I recollect in Lasswade besides the Monday
morning aforesaid is not much. I remember standing
at the smithy with brother Willie, on some occasion
when the big boy was very unwillingly charged to take
his little sister somewhere or other, — standing in the
dark, wondering at the sparks as they flew up and the
dark figures of the smith and his men; and I remember
playing on the road opposite the house, where there was
a low wall over which the Esk and the country beyond
could be seen (I think), playing with two little kittens,
who were called Lord Brougham and Lord Grey. It
must have been immediately after the passing of the
Reform Bill, and I suppose this was why the kittens bore
such names. We were all tremendously political and
Radical, my mother especially and Frank. Likewise I
recollect with the most vivid clearness on what must have
been a warm still summer day, lying on my back in the
grass, the little blue speedwells in which are very distinct

before me, and looking up into the sky. The depths of it, the blueness of it, the way in which it seemed to move and fly and avoid the gaze which could not penetrate beyond that profound unfathomable blue, — the bliss of lying there doing nothing, trying to look into it, growing giddy with the effort, with a sort of vague realisation of the soft swaying of the world in space! I feel the giddiness in my brain still, and the happiness, as if I had been the first discoverer of that wonderful sky. All my little recollections are like pictures to which the meaning, naturally, is put long afterwards. I did not know the world moved or anything about it, being under six at most; but I can feel the sensation of the small head trying to fix that great universe, and in the effort growing dizzy and going round.

We left Lasswade when I was six, my father's business taking him to Glasgow, to the misery of my mother, who was leaving her boys behind her. My father is a very dim figure in all that phantasmagoria. I had to be very quiet in the evenings when he was at home, not to disturb him; and he took no particular notice of me or of any of us. My mother was all in all. How she kept everything going, and comfortably going, on the small income she had to administer, I can't tell ; it seems like a miracle, though of course we lived in the utmost obscurity and simplicity, she herself doing the great part of all that was done in the house. I was the child of her age — not her old age, but the sentiment was the same. She had lost three children one after another — one a girl about whom I used to make all sorts of dream-romances, to the purport that Isabella had never died at all, and was brought back in this or that miraculous way to make my mother and myself supremely happy. I was born after that period of misery, and brought back life to my mother's heart. She was of the old type of Scotch mothers, not demonstrative, not caressing, but I know now that I was a kind of idol to

her from my birth. My clothes were all made by her
tender hands, finer and more beautifully worked than
ever child's clothes were; my under garments fine linen
and trimmed with little delicate laces, to the end that
there might be nothing coarse, nothing less than exquisite, about me; that I might grow up with all the
delicacies of a woman's ideal child.

But she was very quick in temper notwithstanding
this, and was very far from spoiling me. I was not
petted nor called by sweet names. But I know now that
my mere name meant everything to her. I was her
Maggie — what more could mortal speech find to say?
How little one realises the character or individuality of
those who are most near and dear. It is with difficulty
even now that I can analyse or make a character of her.
She herself is there, not any type or variety of human-
kind. She was taller than I am, not so stout as I
have grown. She had a sweet fresh complexion, and a
cheek so soft that I can feel the sensation of putting mine
against it still, and beautiful liquid brown eyes, full of
light and fun and sorrow and anger, flashing and melting,
terrible to look at sometimes when one was in disgrace.
Her teeth projected, when she had teeth, but she lost
and never replaced them, which did not, I think, harm
her looks very much — at least, not in my consciousness.
I am obliged to confess that when I remember her first
she wore a brown front! according to the fashion of the
time — which fashion she detested, and suddenly aban-
doning it one day, appeared with the most lovely white
hair, which gave a charm of harmonious colour to her
beautiful complexion and brown eyes and eyebrows, but
which was looked upon with consternation by her contemporaries, who thought the change wickedness. She
had grown very early grey like myself, but was at this
period, I should think, about forty-five. She wore always a cap with white net quilled closely round her face,
and tied under her chin with white ribbons; and in
winter always a white shawl; her dress cut not quite to

her throat, and a very ample white net or cambric hand-kerchief showing underneath. She had read everything she could lay hands upon all her life, and was fond of quoting Pope, so that we used to call her Popish in after-days when I knew what Popish in this sense meant.

She had entered into everything that was passing all her life with the warmest energy and animation, as was her nature; was Radical and democratic and the highest of aristocrats all in one. She had a very high idea, founded on I have never quite known what, of the importance of the Oliphant family, so that I was brought up with the sense of belonging (by her side) to an old, chivalrous, impoverished race. I have never got rid of the prejudice, though I don't think our branch of the Oliphants was much to brag of. I would not, however, do anything to dispel the delusion, if it is one, for my mother's sake, who held it stoutly and without a doubt. Her father had been a prodigal, and I fear a profligate, whose wife had not been able to bear with him (my mother would have borne anything and everything for her children's sake, to keep their home intact), and her youth had been a troubled and partially dependent one, — dependent upon relations on the one side, whom it was a relief, I suppose, to the high-spirited girl to think as much inferior in race as they were in the generosity and princeliness of nature which was hers. So far as that went she might have been a queen.

I understand the Carlyles, both he and she, by means of my mother as few people appear able to do. She had Mrs Carlyle's wonderful gift of narrative, and she possessed in perfection that dangerous facility of sarcasm and stinging speech which Sir Walter attrib-utes to Queen Mary. Though her kindness was inex-haustible and her love boundless, yet she could drive her opponent of the moment half frantic with half-a-dozen words, and cut to the quick with a flying phrase. On the other side, there was absolutely nothing that she would not have done or endured for her own; and no appeal to her generosity was ever made in vain. She was a poor woman all her life, but her instinct was always to give. And she would have kept open house if she could have had her way, on heaven knows how little a-year. My father was in one way very different. He hated strangers; guests at his table were a bore to him. In his later days he would have nobody invited, or if guests came, retired and would not see them, — but he was not illiberal.

We lived for a long time in Liverpool, where my father had an office in the Custom-house. I don't know exactly what, except that he took affidavits — which was a joke in the house — having a special commission for that purpose. We lived for some time in the North End (no doubt a great deal changed now, and I have known nothing about it for thirty years and more), where there was a Scotch church, chiefly for the use of the engineers and their families who worked in the great foundries. One of the first things I remember here was great distress among the people, on what account I cannot tell — I must have been a girl of thirteen or so, I think. A fund was raised for their relief, of which my father was treasurer, and both my brothers were drawn in to help. This was very momentous in our family, from the fact that it was the means of bringing Frank, up to this time everything that was good except in respect to the Church, to that last and crowning excellence. He got interested about the poor, and began to come with us to church, and filled my mother's cup with happiness. Willie, always careless, always kind, ready to do anything for anybody, but who had already come by some defeat in life which I did not understand, and who was at home idle, took the charge of administering this charity, and used to go about the poor streets with a cart of coal behind him and his pockets stuffed with orders for bread and provisions of all kinds. All this I remem-

ber, I think, more through my mother's keen half
anguish of happiness and pride than through my own
recollection. That he had done so poorly for himself
was bitter, but that he did so well for the poor was
sweet ; oh ! and such a vindication of the bright-eyed,
sweet-tempered unfortunate, who never was anybody's
enemy but his own — words which were more true in
his case than in most others. And then Frank was
busy in the good work too, and at last a member of
the Church, and all well. This is not to say that
there were not domestic gusts at times.

When I was sixteen I began to have — what shall I
say ? — not lovers exactly, except in the singular — but one
or two people about who revealed to me the fact that I
too was like the girls in the poets. I recollect distinctly
the first compliment, though not a compliment in the
ordinary sense of the word, which gave me that bewildering happy sense of being able to touch somebody else's
heart — which was half fun and infinitely amusing, yet
something more. The speaker was a young Irishman,
one of the young ministers that came to our little church,
at that time vacant. He had joined Frank and me on a
walk, and when we were passing and looking at a very
pretty cottage on the slope of the hill at Everton,
embowered in gardens and shrubberies, he suddenly
looked at me and said, " It would be Elysium." I
laughed till I cried at this speech afterwards, though at
the moment demure and startled. But the little incident
remains to me, as so many scenes in my early life do,
like a picture suffused with a soft delightful light: the
glow in the young man's eyes ; the lowered tone and
little speech aside ; the soft thrill of meaning which was
nothing and yet much. Perhaps if I were not a novelist
addicted to describing such scenes, I might not remember
it after — how long ? Forty-one years. What a long
time ! I could not have been sixteen. Then came the
episode of J. Y., which was very serious indeed. We
were engaged on the eve of his going away. He was to

go to America for three years and then return for me.
He was a good, simple, pious, domestic, kind-hearted
fellow, fair-haired, not good-looking, not ideal at all. He
cannot have been at all clever, and I was rather. When
he went away our correspondence for some time was very
full; then I began to find his letters silly, and I suppose
said as much. Then there were quarrels, quarrels with
the Atlantic between, then explanations, and then dreadful silence. It is amusing to look back upon, but it was
not at all amusing to me then. My poor little heart was
broken. I remember another scene without being able
to explain it : my mother and myself walking home from
somewhere — I don't know where — after it was certain
that there was no letter, and that all was over. I think
it was a winter night and rainy, and I was leaning on
her arm, and the blank of the silence, and the dark and
the separation, and the cutting off of all the dreams that
had grown about his name, came over me and seemed to
stop my very life. My poor little heart was broken. I
was just over seventeen, I think.

These were the only breaks in my early life. We lived
in the most singularly secluded way. I never was at a
dance till after my marriage, never went out, never saw
anybody at home. Our pleasures were books of all and
every kind, newspapers and magazines, which formed
the staple of our conversation, as well as all our amusement. In the time of my depression and sadness my
mother had a bad illness, and I was her nurse, or at least
attendant. I had to sit for hours by her bedside and
keep quiet. I had no liking then for needlework, a taste
which developed afterwards, so I took to writing. There
was no particular purpose in my beginning except this,
to secure some amusement and occupation for myself
while I sat by my mother's bedside. I wrote a little book
in which the chief character was an angelic elder sister,
unmarried, who had the charge of a family of motherless
brothers and sisters, and who had a shrine of sorrow in
her life in the shape of the portrait and memory of her

lover who had died young. It was all very innocent and guileless, and my audience — to wit, my mother and brother Frank — were highly pleased with it. (It was published long after by W. on his own account, and very silly I think it is, poor little thing.) I think I was then about sixteen. Afterwards I wrote another very much concerned with the Church business, in which the heroine, I recollect, was a girl, who in the beginning of the story was a sort of half-witted undeveloped creature, but who ended by being one of those lofty poetical beings whom girls love. She was called, I recollect, Ibby, but why, I cannot explain. I had the satisfaction afterwards, when I came to my full growth, of burning the manuscript, which was a three-volume business. I don't think any effort was ever made to get a publisher for it.

We were living at the time in Liverpool, either in a house in Great Homer Street or in Juvenal Street — very classical in point of name but in nothing else. Probably neither of these places exists any longer — very good houses though, at least the last. I have lately described in a letter in the 'St James' Gazette' a curious experience of mine as a child while living in one of these places. It was in the time of the Anti-Corn Law agitation, and I was about fourteen. There was a great deal of talk in the papers, which were full of that agitation, about a petition from women to Parliament upon that subject, with instructions to get sheets ruled for signatures, and an appeal to ladies to help in procuring them. It was just after or about the time of our great charity, and I was in the way of going thus from house to house. Accordingly I got a number of these sheets, or probably Frank got them for me, and set to work. Another girl went with me, I believe, but I forget who she was. The town was all portioned out into districts under the charge of ladies appointed by the committee, but we flung ourselves upon a street, no matter where, and got our papers filled and put all the authorised agents comically out.

B

Nobody could discover who we were. I took my sheets to the meeting of the ladies, and was much wondered at, being to the external eye a child, though to my own consciousness quite a grown-up person. The secretary of the association or committee, or whatever it was, was, I think, a Miss Hayward; at all events her Christian name was Lawrencina, which she wrote L'cina. I admired her greatly, and admired her pretty handwriting and everything about her. I myself wrote abominably, resisting up to this time all efforts to teach me better; but the circulars and notes with Miss L'cina's pretty name developed in me a warm ambition. I began to copy her writing, and mended in my own from that day. It did not come to very much, the printers would say.

I was a tremendous politician in those days.

I forget when it was that we moved to Birkenhead — not, I think, till after the extraordinary epoch of the publication of my first book. From the time above spoken of I went on writing, and somehow, I don't remember how, got into the history of Mrs Margaret Maitland. There had been some sketches from life in the story which, as I have said, I burned; but that was pure imagination. A slight reflection of my own childhood perhaps was in the child Grace, a broken bit of reflection here and there from my mother in the picture of Mrs Margaret. Willie, after many failures and after a long illness, which we were in hopes had purified him from all his defects, had gone to London to go through some studies at the London University and in the College called the English Presbyterian, to which in our warm Free Churchism we had attached ourselves. He took my MS. to Colburn, then one of the chief publishers of novels, and for some weeks nothing was heard of it, when one morning came a big blue envelope containing an agreement by which Mr Colburn pledged himself to publish my book on the half-profit system, accompanied by a letter from a Mr S. W. Fullom, full of compliments as to its originality, &c. I have forgotten the terms now, but then I knew them by heart. The delight, the astonishment, the amusement of this was not to be described. First and foremost, it was the most extraordinary joke that ever was. Maggie's story! My mother laughed and cried with pride and happiness and amazement unbounded. She thought Mr S. W. Fullom a great authority and a man of genius, and augured the greatest advantage to me from his acquaintance and that of all the great literary persons about him. This wonderful event must have come most fortunately to comfort the family under new trouble; for things had again gone wrong with poor Willie — he had fallen once more into his old vice and debt and misery. He had still another term in London before he finished the course of study he was engaged in; and when the time came for his return I was sent with him to take care of him. It was almost the first time I had ever been separated from my mother. One visit of two or three weeks to the Hasties of Fairy Knowe, which had its part too in my little development, had been my only absence from home ; and how my mother made up her mind to this three months' parting I do not know, but for poor Willie's sake everything was possible. We had lodgings near Bruton Crescent in a street where our cousins, Frank and Tom Oliphant, were in the same house. We had the parlour, I remember, where I sat in the mornings when Willie was at his lectures. Afterwards he came in and I went out with him to walk. We used to walk through all the curious little passages leading, I believe, to Holborn, and full of old bookshops, which were our delight. And he took me to see the parks and various places — though not those to which I should suppose a girl from the country would be taken. The bookshops are the things I remember best. He was as good as he could be, docile and sweet-tempered and never rebellious ; and I was a little dragon watching over him with remorseless anxiety. I discovered, I remember, a trifling bill which had not been included when his debts were paid, and I took my small fierce measures that it should never reach my mother's ears, nor trouble her. I ordained that for two days in the week we should give up our mid-day meal and make up at the evening one, which we called supper, for the want of it. On these days, accordingly, he did not come home, or came only to fetch me, and we went out for a long walk, sustaining ourselves with a bun until it should be time to come home to tea. He agreed to this ordinance without a murmur — my poor, good, tender-hearted, simple-minded Willie; and the little bill was paid and never known of at home.

Curiously enough, I remember little of the London sights or of any impression they made upon me. We knew scarcely anybody. Mrs Hamilton, the sister of Edward Irving's wife and a relation, took some notice of us, but she was almost the only individual I knew. And my heart was too full of my charge to think much of the cousin up-stairs with whom my fate was soon to be connected. We had known scarcely anything of each other before. We were new acquaintances, though relations. He took me, I remember, to the National Gallery, full of of expectation as to the effect the pictures would have upon me. And I — was struck dumb with disappointment. I had never seen any pictures. I can't tell what I expected to see — something that never was on sea or shore. My ideal of absolute ignorance was far too high-flown, I suppose, for anything human. I was horribly disappointed, and dropped down from untold heights of imagination to a reality I could not understand. I remember, in the humiliation of my downfall, and in the sense of my cousin's astonished disappointment at my want of appreciation, fixing upon a painting — a figure of the Virgin in a Crucifixion, I think by Correggio, but I am quite vague about it — as the thing I liked best. I chose that as Words-worth's little boy put forth the weathercock at Kilve

— in despair at my own incapacity to admire. I remember also the heads of the old Jews in Leonardo's Christ in the Temple. The face of the young Redeemer with its elaborate crisped hair shocked me with a sense of profanity, but the old heads I could believe in. And that was all I got out of my first glimpse into the world of art. I cannot recollect whether it was then or after, that an equally great disillusionment in the theatre befell me. The play was "Twelfth Night," and the lovely beginning of that play —

" That strain again! it had a dying fall"

— was given by a nobody in white tights lying on a sofa and balancing a long leg as he spoke. The disgust, the disenchantment, the fury remain in my mind now. Once more I came tumbling down from my ideal and all my anticipations. Mrs Charles Kean was Viola, and she was middle-aged and stout![1] I was more than disappointed, I was angry and disgusted and cast down. What was the good of anything if that was all that Shakespeare and the great Masters could come to?

I remember after this a day at Greenwich and Woolwich, and the sight of the Arsenal, though why that should have made an impression on my memory, heaven knows! I remember the pyramids of balls, and some convicts whose appearance gave me a thrill of horror, — I think they were convicts, though why convicts should be at Woolwich I can't tell — perhaps it was a mistake. And then Mr Colburn kindly I thought most kindly, and thanked him *avec effusion* — gave me £150 for 'Margaret Maitland.' I remember walking along the street with delightful elation, thinking that, after all, I was worth something — and not to be hustled about. I remember, too, getting the first review of my book in the twilight of a wintry dark afternoon, and reading it by the firelight — always half-amused at

[1] Probably under thirty. — ED.

the thought that it was *me* who was being thus discussed in the newspapers.   It was the 'Athenæum,'
and it was on the whole favourable. Of course this
event preceded by a couple of months the transaction
with Mr Colburn.   I think the book was in its third
edition before he offered me that £150.   I remember
no reviews except that one of the 'Athenæum,' nor
any particular effect which my success produced in me,
except that sense of elation.   I cannot think why the
book succeeded so well.   When I read it over some
years after, I felt nothing but shame at its foolish little
polemics and opinions.   I suppose there must have been
some breath of' youth and sincerity in it which touched
people, and there had been no Scotch stories for a
long time.   Lord Jeffrey, then an old man and very
near his end, sent me a letter of sweet praise, which
filled my mother with rapture and myself with an
abashed gratitude.   I was very young.   Oddly enough,
it has always remained a matter of doubt with me
whether the book was published in 1849 or 1850.   I
thought the former; but Geraldine Macpherson, whom
I met in London for the first time a day or two before
it was published, declared it to be 1850, from the fact
that *that* was the year of her marriage.   If a woman
remembers any date, it must be the date of her marriage![1] so I don't doubt Geddie was right.   Anyhow,
if it was 1850, I was then only twenty-two, and in
some things very young for my age, as in others perhaps older than my years.   I was wonderfully little
moved by the business altogether.   I had a great
pleasure in writing, but the success and the three edi-
tions had no particular effect upon my mind.   For
one thing, I saw very few people. We had no society.
My father had a horror of strangers, and would never
see any one who came to the house, which was a continual wet blanket to my mother's cordial, hospitable
nature; but she had given up struggling long before

[1] It *was* 1849.— ED.

my time, and I grew up without any idea of the
pleasures and companions of youth. I did not know
them, and therefore did not miss them; but I daresay
this helped to make me — not indifferent, rather unconscious, of what might in other circumstances have
"turned my head." My head was as steady as a rock.
I had nobody to praise me except my mother and
Frank, and their applause — well, it was delightful, it
was everything in the world — it was life, — but it did
not count. They were part of me, and I of them,
and we were all in it. After a while it came to be
the custom that I should every night "read what I
had written" to them before I went to bed. They
were very critical sometimes, and I felt while I was
reading whether my little audience was with me or
not, which put a good deal of excitement into the
performance. But that was all the excitement I had.

I began another book called 'Caleb Field,' about the
Plague in London, the very night I had finished 'Margaret Maitland.' I had been reading Defoe, and got
the subject into my head. It came to one volume only,
and I took a great deal of trouble about a Noncon-
formist minister who spoke in antitheses very carefully
constructed. I don't think it attracted much notice,
but I don't remember. Other matters, events even of
our uneventful life, took so much more importance in
life than these books — nay, it must be a kind of affec-
tation to say that, for the writing ran through everything. But then it was also subordinate to everything,
to be pushed aside for any little necessity. I had no
table even to myself, much less a room to work in,
but sat at the corner of the family table with my writ-
ing-book, with everything going on as if I had been
making a shirt instead of writing a book. Our rooms
in those days were sadly wanting in artistic arrange-
ment. The table was in the middle of the room, the
centre round which everybody sat with the candles or
lamp upon it. My mother sat always at needle-work

of some kind, and talked to whoever might be present, and I took my share in the conversation, going on all the same with my story, the little groups of imaginary persons, these other talks evolving themselves quite undisturbed. It would put me out now to have some one sitting at the same table talking while I worked — at least I would think it put me out, with that sort of conventionalism which grows upon one. But up to this date, 1888, I have never been shut up in a separate room, or hedged off with any observances. My study, all the study I have ever attained to, is the little second drawing-room where all the (feminine) life of the house goes on; and I don't think I have ever had two hours undisturbed (except at night, when everybody is in bed) during my whole literary life. Miss Austen, I believe, wrote in the same way, and very much for the same reason; but at her period the natural flow of life took another form. The family were half ashamed to have it known that she was not just a young lady like the others, doing her embroidery. Mine were quite pleased to magnify me, and to be proud of my work, but always with a hidden sense that it was an admirable joke, and no idea that any special facilities or retirement was necessary. My mother, I believe, would have felt her pride and rapture much checked, almost humiliated, if she had conceived that I stood in need of any artificial aids of that or any other description. That would at once have made the work unnatural to her eyes, and also to mine. I think the first time I ever secluded myself for my work was years after it had become my profession and sole dependence — when I was living after my widowhood in a relation's house, and withdrew with my book and my inkstand from the family drawing-room out of a little conscious ill-temper which made me feel guilty, notwithstanding that the retirement was so very justifiable! But I did not feel it to be so, neither did the companions from whom I withdrew.

After this period our poor Willie became a minister

of the English Presbyterian Church, then invested with glory by the Free Church, its real parent, which in our fervid imagination we had by this time dressed up with all sorts of traditional splendour. It, we flattered ourselves, was the direct successor of the two thousand seceders of 1661 (was that the date?). There had been a downfall, we allowed, into Unitarianism and indifference; but this was the real, and a very respectable, tradition. Willie went to a very curious little place in the wilds of Northumberland, where my mother and I decided — with hopes strangely wild, it seems to me now, after all that had gone before — that he was at length to do well and be as strenuous to his duty as he was gentle in temper and tender in heart. Poor Willie! It was a sort of show village with pretty flowery cottages and gardens, in a superior one of which he lived, or rather lodged, the income being very small and the position humble. It was, however, so far as my recollection goes, sufficiently like a Scotch parish to convince us that the church and parsonage were quite exotic, and the humble chapel the real religious centre of the place. A great number of the people were, I believe, Presbyterians, and the continuance of their worship and little strait ceremony undoubted from the time of the Puritans, though curiously enough the minister was known to his flock by the title of the priest. I don't in the least recollect what the place was like, yet a whiff of the rural air tinged with peat or wood, and of the roses with which the cottages were garlanded, and an impression of the subdued light through the greenish small window half veiled in flowers, remains with me, — very sweet, homely, idyllic, like something in a pathetic country story of peace overshadowed with coming trouble. There was a shadow of a ruined castle in the background, I think Norham; but all is vague, — I have not the clear memory of what I saw in my youth that many people retain. I see a little collection of pictures, but the background is all vague. The only vehicle we could get to take us to Berwick was, I recollect, a cart, carefully arranged with straw-covered sacking to make us comfortable. The man who drove it was very anxious to be engaged and taken with us as "Miss Wilson's coachman." Why mine, or why we should have taken a rustic "Jockey-to-the-fair" for a coachman, if we had wanted such an article, I don't know. I suppose there must have been some sort of compliment implied to my *beaux yeux*, or I should not have remembered this. We left Willie with thankful hearts, yet an ache of fear. Surely in that peaceful humble quiet, with those lowly sacred duties and all his goodness and kindness, he would do well! I don't remember how long it continued. So long as he kept up the closest correspondence, writing every second day and giving a full account of himself, there was an uneasy satisfaction at home. But there is always a prophetic ache in the heart when such calamity is on the way.

One day, without warning, except that his letters had begun to fail a little, my mother received an anonymous letter about him. She went off that evening, travelling all night to Edinburgh, which was the quickest way, and then to Berwick. She was very little used to travelling, and she was over sixty, which looked a great age then. I suppose the trains were slower in those days, for I know she got to Edinburgh only in the morning, and then had to go on by the other line to Berwick, and then drive six miles to the village, where she found all the evil auguries fulfilled, and poor Willie fallen again helpless into that Slough of Despond. She remained a few miserable days, and then brought him back with her, finally defeated in the battle which he was quite unfit to wage. He must have been then, I think, about thirty-three, in the prime of strength and youth; but except for a wavering and uncertain interval now and then, he never got out of the mire nor was able to support himself again. I remember the horrible moment of his coming home. Frank and I went down, I suppose, to the ferry at Birkenhead to meet the travellers. We were all very grave — not a word of reproach did any one say, but to be cheerful, to talk about nothing, was impossible. We drove up in silence to the house where we lived, asking a faint question now and then about the journey. I remember that Willie had a little dog called Brownie with him, and the relief this creature was, which did not understand being shut up in the carriage and made little jumps at the window, and had to be petted and restrained. Brownie brought a little movement, an involuntary laugh at his antics, to break the horrible silence — an angel could scarcely have done more for us. When we got home there was the settling down in idleness, the hopeless decision of any wretched possibility there might be for him. The days and weeks and months in which he smoked and read old novels and the papers, and, most horrible of all, got to content himself with that life! The anguish in all our hearts looking at him, not knowing what to do, sometimes assailed by gusts of impatience, always closing down in the hopelessness of it; the incapacity to find or suggest anything, the dreary spectacle of that content is before me, with almost as keen a sense of the misery as if it had been yesterday.

I had been in the habit of copying out carefully, quite proud of my neat MS., all my books, now becoming a recognized feature of the family life. It struck us all as a fine idea that Willie might copy them for me, and retrieve a sort of fictitious independence by getting 10 per cent upon the price of them; and I really think he felt quite comfortable on this. Of course, the sole use of the copying was the little corrections and improvements I made in going over my work again.

It was after this that my cousin Frank came upon a

visit. We had seen, and yet had not seen, a great deal
of each other in London during the three months I had
spent there with Willie ; but my mind had been preoccupied with Willie chiefly, and a little with my book.
When Frank made me the extraordinary proposal for
which I was totally unprepared, that we should, as he
said, build up the old Drumthwacket together, my only
answer was an alarmed negative, the idea never having
entered my mind. But in six months or so things
changed. It is not a matter into which I can enter
here.

In the spring of 1851 my mother and I were in
Edinburgh, and there made the acquaintance of the
Wilsons, our second cousins, — George Wilson being at
that time Professor of something which meant chemistry,
but was not called so. His mother was an exceedingly
bright, vivacious old lady, a universal devourer of books,
and with that kind of scientific tendency which made her
encourage her boys to form museums, and collect fossils,
butterflies, &c. I forget how my mother and she got on,
but I always liked her.

George Wilson was an excellent talker, full of banter
and a kind of humour, full of ability, too, I believe,
writing very amusing letters and talking very amusing
talk, which was all the more credit to him as he was in
very bad health, kept alive by the fact that he could
eat, and so maintain a modicum of strength — enough
to get on by. There were two daughters — Jessie and
Jeanie — the younger of whom became my brother
Frank's wife; and the eldest son, who was married,
lived close by, and was then, I think, doing literary
work for Messrs Nelson, reading for them and advising
them about books. He very soon after this migrated
to Canada, and became eventually President of University College, Toronto, and Sir Daniel in the end of
his life.

My mother at this time renewed acquaintance with
Dr Moir of Musselburgh, an old friend of hers, who had,

I believe, attended me when, as a very small child, I fell
into the fire, or rather against the bars of the grate,
marking my arm in a way which it never recovered.
This excellent man, whom everybody loved, was the
Delta of 'Blackwood's Magazine,' and called everywhere
by that name. He had written much gentle poetry, and
one story à la Galt called 'Mansie Wauch,' neither of
which were good enough for him, yet got him a certain
reputation, especially some pathetic verses about children
he had lost, which went to the heart of every mother who
had lost children, my own mother first and foremost.
He had married a very handsome stately lady, a little
conventional, but with an unfailing and ready kindness
which often made her mannerisms quite gracious and
beautiful. There was already a handsome daughter
married, though under twenty, and many other fine, tall,
well-bred, handsome creatures, still in long hair and short
skirts, growing up. I think I was left behind to pay a
visit when my mother returned home, and then had a
kind of introduction to Edinburgh literary society, in one
case very important for myself. For in one expedition
we made, Major Blackwood, one of the publishing firm,
and brother of the editor of the 'Magazine,' was of the
party; and my long connection with his family thus
began. He was accompanied by a young man, a Mr
Cupples, of whom, except his name, I have no recollection, but who was the author of a sea-story then, I think,
going on in 'Blackwood,' called the 'Green Hand,' and
who, it was hoped, would be as successful as the author
of 'Tom Cringle' and the 'Cruise of the Midge,' who had
been a very effective contributor twenty years before.
All I remember of him was that my cousin Daniel
Wilson, who was also of the party, indignantly pointed
out to me the airs which this young author gave himself,
"as if it was such a great thing to be a contributor to
'Blackwood'!" I am afraid I thought it *was* a great
thing, and had not remarked the young author's airs;
but Daniel was of the opposite camp. Major Blackwood,

who interested me most, was a mild soldierly man, with the gentlest manners and drooping eyelids, which softened his look, or so at least it appears to me at the end of so many years.

I remember that one of the places we visited was Wallyford, where was the house in which I was born, but of which I had no recollection. It must have been a pleasant homely house, with a projecting half turret enclosing the staircase, as in many houses in the Lothians, the passages and kitchen down-stairs floored with red brick, and a delightful large low drawing-room above, with five greenish windows looking out upon Arthur's Seat in the distance, and a ghost of Edinburgh.[1] That room charmed me greatly, and in after days I used to think of becoming its tenant and living there, for the sake of the landscape and the associations and that pretty old room ; but before I could have carried out such an idea, even had it been more real than a fancy, the pretty house was pulled down, and a square, aggressive, and very commonplace new farmhouse built in its place.

The consequence of my introduction to Major Blackwood was, that some time in the course of the following months I sent him the manuscript of my story ' Katie Stewart ' : a little romance of my mother's family, gleaned from her recollections and descriptions. The scene of this story was chiefly laid in old Kellie Castle, which I was not then aware was the home of our own ancestors, from whom it had passed long before into the hands of the Erskines, Earls of Kellie — with the daughter of which house Katie Stewart had been brought up. She was my mother's great-aunt, and had lived to a great age. She had seen Prince Charlie enter Edinburgh, and had told all her experiences to my mother, who told them to me, so that I never was quite sure whether I had not been Katie Stewart's contemporary in my own

[1] This house is the scene of the story of 'Isabel Dysart,' reprinted since Mrs Oliphant's death. — ED.

person. And this was her love-tale. I received proofs
of this story on the morning of my wedding-day, and
thus my connection with the firm of Blackwood began.
They were fond of nicknames, and I was known among
them by the name of "Katie" for a long time, as I
discovered lately (1896) in some old letters. I suppose
they thought me so young and simple (as they say in
these letters) that the girl's name was appropriate to me.
I was not tall ("middle height" we called it in those
days), and very inexperienced, — "so simple and yet self-
possessed," I am glad to say Major Blackwood reports
of me. I was only conscious of being dreadfully *shy*.

We were married in Birkenhead on the 4th May 1852,
— and the old home, which had come to consist of
such incongruous elements, was more or less broken up.
My brother Frank, discontented and wounded partly
by my marriage, partly by the determination to abandon
him and follow me to London, which my father and
mother had formed, married too, hastily, but very successfully in a way as it turned out, and so two new
houses were formed out of the partial ruins of the old.
Had the circumstances been different — had they stayed
in Birkenhead and I gone alone with my husband to
London — some unhappiness might have been spared.
Who can tell? There would have been other unhappiness
to take its place. They settled in a quaint little house in
a place called Park Village, old-fashioned, semi-rustic,
and pretty enough, with a long strip of garden stretching
down to the edge of a deep cutting of the railway, where
we used to watch the trains passing far below. The
garden was gay with flowers, quantities of brilliant
poppies of all colours I remember, which I liked for the
colour and hated for the heavy ill odour of them, and
the sensation as of evil flowers. Our house in Harrington Square was very near: it looked all happy enough
but was not, for my husband and my mother did not
get on. My father sat passive, taking no notice, with
his paper, not perceiving much, I believe.

My child's birth made a momentary gleam of joy soon lost in clouds.

My mother became ailing and concealed it, and kept alive — or at least kept her last illness off by sheer stress of will until my second child was born a year and a day after the first. She was with me, but sank next day into an illness from which she never rose. She died in September 1854, suffering no attendance but mine, though she concealed from me how ill she was for a long time. I remember the first moment in which I had any real fear, speaking to the doctor with a sudden impulse, in the front of her door, all in a green shade with the waving trees, demanding his real opinion. I do not think I had any understanding of the gravity of the circumstances. He shook his head, and I knew — the idea having never entered my mind before that she was to die. I recollect going away, walking home as in a dream, not able to go to her, to look at her, from whom I had never had a secret, with this secret in my soul that must be told least of all to her; and the sensation that here was something which would not lighten after a while as all my troubles had always done, and pass away. I had never come face to face with the inevitable before. But there was no daylight here — no hope — no getting over it. Then there followed a struggle of a month or two, much suffering on her part, and a long troubled watch and nursing on mine. At the very end I remember the struggle against overwhelming sleep, after nights and days in incessant anxiety, which made me so bitterly ashamed of the limits of wretched nature. To want to sleep while she was dying seemed so unnatural and horrible. I never had come within sight of death before. And, oh me! when all was over, mingled with my grief there was — how can I say it? — something like a dreadful relief.

Within a few months after, my little Marjorie, my second child, died on the 8th February; and then with deep shame and anguish I felt what I suppose was another wretched limit of nature. My dearest mother, who had been everything to me all my life, and to whom I was everything; the companion, friend, counsellor, minstrel, story-teller, with whom I had never wanted for constant interest, entertainment, and fellowship, — did not give me, when she died, a pang so deep as the loss of the little helpless baby, eight months old. I miss my mother till this moment when I am nearly as old as she was (sixty, 10th June 1888); I think instinctively still of asking her something, referring to her for information, and I dream constantly of being a girl with her at home. But at that moment her loss was nothing to me in comparison with the loss of my little child.

I lost another infant after that, a day old. My spirit sank completely under it. I used to go about saying to myself, "A little while and ye shall not see me," with a longing to get to the end and have all safe — for my one remaining, my eldest, my Maggie seemed as if she too must be taken out of my arms. People will say it was an animal instinct perhaps. Neither of these little ones could speak to me or exchange an idea or show love, and yet their withdrawal was like the sun going out from the sky — life remained, the daylight continued, but all was different. It seems strange to me now at this long distance — but so it was.

The glimpse of society I had during my married life in London was not of a very elevating kind; or perhaps I — with my shyness and complete unacquaintance with the ways of people who gave parties and paid incessant visits — was only unable to take any pleasure in it, or get beyond the outside petty view, and the same strange disappointment and disillusion with which the pictures and the stage had filled me, bringing down my ridiculous impossible ideal to the ground. I have tried to illustrate my youthful feelings about this several times in words. I had expected everything that was superlative — beautiful conversation, all about books and the finest subjects, great people whose notice would be an

C

honour, poets and painters, and all the sympathy of congenial minds, and the feast of reason and the flow of soul. But it is needless to say I found none of these things. We went " out," not very often, to parties where there was always a good deal of the literary element, but of a small kind, and where I found everything very commonplace and poor, not at all what I expected. I never did myself any justice, as a certain little lion-hunter, a Jewish patroness of the arts, who lived somewhere in the region about Harley Street, said. That is to say, I got as quickly as I could into a corner and stood there, rather wistfully wishing to know people, but not venturing to make any approach, waiting till some one should speak to me ; which much exasperated my aspiring hostess, who had picked me up as a new novelist, and meant me to help to amuse her guests, which I had not the least idea how to do. I fear I must have been rather exasperating to my husband, who was more given to society than I, and tried in vain (as I can now see) to form me and make me attend to my social duties, which even in such a small matter as returning calls I was terribly neglectful of — out of sheer shyness and gaucherie, I think ; for I was always glad and grateful when anybody would insist on making friends with me, as a few people did. There was an old clergyman, Mr Laing, who did, I remember, and more or less his wife — he especially. He liked me, I think, and complimented me by saying he did not like literary ladies — a sort of thing people are rather disposed to say to me. And Lance (the painter of fruits and flowers and still life), who was a wit in his way, was also a great friend of mine. He dared me to put him in a book, and I took him at his word and did so, making a very artless representation, and using some of his own stories ; so that everybody recognised the sketch, which was done in mere fun and liking, and pleased him very much — the only actual bit of real life I ever took for a book. It was in ' Zaidee,' I think.

Among my literary acquaintances was the Mr Fullom who had read for old Colburn my first book, and whose acquaintance as an eminent literary man and great notability we had all thought at home it would be such a fine thing to make. He turned out a very small personage indeed, a solemn man, with a commonplace wife, people whom it was marvellous to think of as intellectual. He wrote a book called 'The Marvels of Science,' a dull piece of manufacture, for which by some wonderful chance he received a gold medal, *Für Kunst*, from the King of Hanover. I think I see him moving solemnly about the little drawing-room with this medal on the breast, and the wife following him. He soon stalked away into the unknown, and I saw him no more. I forget how I became acquainted with the S. C. Halls, who used to ask me to their parties, and who were literary people of the most prominent and conventional type, rather satisfying to the sense on the whole, as the sort of thing one expected. Mrs Hall had retired upon the laurels got by one or two Irish novels, and was surrounded by her husband with the atmosphere of admiration, which was the right thing for a "fair" writer. He took her very seriously, and she accepted the *rôle*, though without, I think, any particular setting up of her own standard. I used to think and say that she looked at me inquisitively, a little puzzled to know what kind of humbug I was, all being humbugs. But she was a kind woman all the same; and I never forget the sheaf of white lilies she sent us for my child's christening, for which I feel grateful still. He was certainly a humbug of the old mellifluous Irish kind — the sort of man whose specious friendlinesses, compliments, and "blarney" were of the most innocent kind, not calculated to deceive anybody, but always amusing. He told Irish stories capitally.

They had the most wonderful collection of people at their house, and she would stand and smile and shake hands, till one felt she must stiffen so, and had lost all consciousness who anybody was. He on his side was never tired, always insinuating, jovial, affectionate. It was at their house, I think, that we met the Howitts — Mary Howitt, a mild, kind, delightful woman, who frightened me very much, I remember, by telling me of many babies whom she had lost through some defective valve in the heart, which she said was somehow connected with too much mental work on the part of the mother, — a foolish thing, I should think, yet the same thing occurred twice to myself. It alarmed and saddened me terribly — but I liked her greatly. Not so her husband, who did not please me at all. For a short time we met them everywhere in our small circle, and then they too disappeared, going abroad, I think. There was a great deal about spiritualism (so called) in the air at this time — its first development in England, — and the Howitts' eldest daughter was an art medium producing wonderful scribble-scrabbles, which it was the wonder of wonders to find her mother, so full of sense and truth, so genuine herself, full of enthusiasm about.

I remember a day at the Halls, which must have been in the summer of 1853. They had then a pretty house at Addleston, near Chertsey. My husband and I travelled down by train in company with a dark, dashing person, an American lady, whom, on arriving at the station, we found to be going to the Halls too. She and I were put into their brougham to drive there, while the gentlemen walked; and she did what she could in a patronising way to find out who I was. She thought me, I supposed, the poor little shy wife of some artist, whom the Halls were being kind to, or something of that humble kind. She turned out to be a literary person of great pretensions, calling herself Grace Greenwood, though that was not her real name, — and I was amused to find a paragraph about myself, as "a little homely Scotchwoman," in the book which she wrote when she got back. Two incidents of this entertainment remain very clear in my memory. One was, that being placed at table beside Mr Frost, the academician, who was

very deaf and very gentle and kind, I was endeavouring
with many mental struggles to repeat to him something
that had produced a laugh, and which his wistful look had
asked to understand, when suddenly one of those hushes
which sometimes come over a large company occurred,
and my voice came out distinct — to my own horrified
consciousness, at least — a sound of terror and shame
to me. The other was, that Gavan Duffy, one of the
recent Irish rebels, and my husband began to discuss,
I suppose, national characteristics, or what they believed
to be such, when the Irishman mentioned gravely and
with some heat that the frolic and the wit usually
attributed to his countrymen were a mere popular delusion, while the Scotchman with equal earnestness
repudiated the caution and prudence ascribed to his
race; which was whimsical enough to be remembered.

Another recollection of one of the Halls' evening
parties in town at a considerably later period rises
like a picture before me. They were fond of every
kind of lion and wonder, great and small. Rosa Bonheur, then at the height of her reputation, was there
one evening, a round-faced, good-humoured woman,
with hair cut short and divided at one side like a man's,
and indeed not very distinct in the matter of sex so far
as dress and appearance went. There was there also a
Chinese mandarin in full costume, smiling blandly upon
the company; and accompanied by a missionary, who had
the charge of him. By some means or other the Chinaman was made to sing what we were informed was a senti-
mental ballad, exceedingly touching and romantic. It was
like nothing so much as the howl of a dog, one of those
grave pieces of canine music which my poor old New-
foundland used to give forth when his favourite organ-
grinder came into the street. (Merry's performance
was the most comical thing imaginable. There was
one organ among many which touched his tenderest
feelings. When it appeared once a-week, he rushed to
it, seated himself beside the man, listened till rapture

and sentiment were wound up to the highest pitch,
and then, lifting up his nose and his voice to heaven,
— sang. There could be no doubt that the dear dog
was giving forth all the poetry of his being in that
appalling noise, — his emotion, his sentiment, his profound seriousness were indisputable, while any human
being within reach was overwhelmed and helpless with
laughter.) The Chinaman sang exactly like Merry, with
the same effect. Rosa Bonheur, I suppose, was more
civil than *nous autres*, and her efforts to restrain the
uncontrollable laugh were superhuman. She almost
swallowed her handkerchief in the effort to conceal it.
I can see her as in a picture, the central figure, with
her bushy short hair, and her handkerchief in her mouth.
All my recollections are like pictures, not continuous, only
a scene detached and conspicuous here and there.

Miss Muloch was another of the principal figures per-
ceptible in the somewhat dimmed panorama of that far-
off life. Her friends the Lovells lived in Mornington
Crescent, which was close to our little house in Harrington Square, — all in a remote region near Regent's Park,
upon the Hampstead Road, where it seems very strange
to me we should have lived, and which, I suppose, is
dreadfully shabby and out-of-the-way. Perhaps it was
shabby then, one's ideas change so greatly. Miss
Muloch lived in a small house in a street a little
farther off even in the wilds than ours. She was a tall
young woman with a slim pliant figure, and eyes that
had a way of fixing the eyes of her interlocutor in a
manner which did not please my shy fastidiousness. It
was embarrassing, as if she meant to read the other upon
whom she gazed, — a pretension which one resented. It
was merely, no doubt, a fashion of what was the intense
school of the time. Mrs Browning did the same thing the
only time I met her, and this to one quite indisposed to
be read. But Dinah was always kind, enthusiastic, somewhat didactic and apt to teach, and much looked up
to by her little band of young women. She too had

little parties, at one of which I remember Miss Cushman, the actress, in a deep recitative, without any apparent tune in it, like the voice of a skipper at sea I thought it, giving forth Kingsley's song of "The Sands of Dee." I was rather afraid of the performer, though long afterwards she came to see me in Paris when I was in much sorrow, and her tenderness and feeling gave me the sensation of suddenly meeting a friend in the darkness, of whose existence there I had no conception. There used to be also at Miss Muloch's parties an extraordinary being in a wheeled chair, with an imperfect face (as if it had been somehow left unfinished in the making), a Mr Smedley, a terrible cripple, supposed to be kept together by some framework of springs and supports, of whom the story was told that he had determined, though the son of a rich man, to maintain himself, and make himself a reputation, and had succeeded in doing both, as the writer — of all things in the world — of sporting novels. He was the author of 'Lewis Arundel' and 'Frank Fairleigh,' both I believe athletic books, and full of feats of horsemanship and strength; which was sufficiently pathetic — though the appearance of this poor man somewhat frightened me too.

Mr Lovell, the father of one of Miss Muloch's chief friends, was the author of "The Wife's Secret," a play lately revived, and which struck me when I saw it as one of the most conventional and unreal possible, very curious to come out of that sober city man. All the guests at these little assemblies were something of the same kind. One looked at them rather as one looked at the figures in Madame Tussaud's, wondering if they were waxwork or life — wondering in the other case whether the commonplace outside might not cover a painter or a poet or something equally fine — whose ethereal qualities were all invisible to the ordinary eye.

What I liked best in the way of society was when we went out occasionally quite late in the evening, Frank and I, after he had left off work in his studio, and went to the house of another painter uninvited, unexpected, always welcome, — I with my work. Alexander Johnstone's house was the one to which we went most. I joined the wife in her little drawing-room, while he went up-stairs to the studio. (They all had the drawing-room proper of the house, the first-floor room, for their studios.) We women talked below of our subjects, as young wives and young mothers do — with a little needle-work and a little gossip. The men above smoked and talked their subjects, investigating the picture of the moment, going over it with advice and criticism; no doubt giving each other their opinions of other artists and other pictures too. And then we supped, frugally, cheerfully, and if there was anything of importance in the studio the wives went up to look at it, or see what progress it had made since the last time, after supper. And then we walked home again. They paid us a return visit some days after of just the same kind. If I knew them now, which I no longer do, I would ask them to dinner, and they me, and most likely we would not enjoy it at all. But those simple evenings were very pleasant. Our whole life was upon very simple lines at this period: we dined in the middle of the day, and our little suppers were not of a kind to require elaborate preparation if another pair came in unexpectedly. It was true society in its way. Nothing of the kind seems possible now.

II.

January 18, 1891.

I FORGET where I left off in this pitiful little record of my life. It was with an attempt to remember somebody worth telling about in the old life in London. We began our housekeeping in Harrington Square, on the way to Camden Town, I think, whereabouts a number of artists had established themselves; though I remember at this moment only the Pickersgills, and not even them very well. Then my Maggie was born, and my dear mother, then still living, had the joy and delight of her grandchild, the third Margaret, — one pleasure at least in that dreary ending of her life. I remember saying that there had been always something wanting to my mother, which I had felt without knowing what it was, till I saw her with my baby in her dear arms. Maggie was always a beautiful child. My dear little Marjorie was always pale and delicate, but with glorious eyes—to think of an eight months' old baby having these! But I remember that as she died she opened them widely and seemed to fix them on me as she lay on my knee, giving up her little soul in that look of consciousness, as it appeared to me. That was in 1855, thirty-six years ago, but I have never forgot the look with which that baby died.

After this we removed to Ulster Place, a larger house, which is the house in London upon which my mind dwells. I pass it sometimes going to King's Cross, when we have gone to Scotland, and a strange fantastic thought crossed my mind the first time I did so in these latter years, as if I might go up to the door and go in and find the old life going on, and see my husband coming down the road, and my little children returning from their walk. There was a kind of feeling of increasing prosperity when we went to that house, more feeling than reality; and I tried to make it pretty, though I fear it would have looked rather dreadful to the ideas of this changed time. It is at the corner of Ulster Place, looking down Harley Street, and next to a large square house with gardens, in which the Oudh princesses or begums lived when they came to England to plead their cause. Some of our windows looked over this garden, and we had glimpses of the strange Eastern figures flitting about—the white robes and shawls, and gleaming ornaments and dusky faces. Later Frank took a small house farther up the road near Baker Street, I think, to make a studio, and began to have his painted windows executed there under his own superintendence, partly because he was not satisfied with the way in which his designs were carried out, partly with the hope that he might then get into a substantial business, instead of precarious artist-work. There was a brightness and hopefulness about the beginning. We were both sanguine, and he dreamed of work that might go on under his eye and keep our household going, while he might return to his painting, which was the work he loved best. So things went on very brightly for a time. He painted his King Richard picture, which was sold for a tolerable price; and then that of the Prodigal, which I have still, and which I think a very touching picture. And orders came in for windows. And, best of all, our delightful boy was born. Ah, me! If I had continued this narrative at the time when I broke it off in 1888, I should have told of this event and all its pleasantness, if not with a light heart, yet without the sudden tears that blind me now, so that I cannot see the page. My beautiful delightful child, with all the little jests, that he had come too late for church, and so was unpunctual all his life after; my Sunday child, "blythe and bonny and happy and gay," as the old rhyme says. I was very anxious at his birth because of the two babies I had lost, and had implored the doctor, my old, kind, cranky Dr Allison, to examine him and tell me honestly if all was well with him. "That fellow!" he said; "he has lungs like a sponge." How well I remember the room, the doctor's look, the baby that had brought joy with him, the flood of ease and happiness that came into my heart. The child was health itself, and vigour and sweetness and life. He was born on Sunday, November 16, 1856. And that winter was a happy and cheerful one. Sebastian Evans, then a fine young fellow fresh from Cambridge, turned aside from the current of his life because of the "doubts," then becoming a fashionable malady, which would not let him go into the Church, and drifting a little, not knowing what to do, came about a window, a memorial to his father; and he and Frank taking to each other, remained as an assistant to help with the cartoons, and by-and-by with the idea of being a partner and sharing the business. He is mixed in all this cheerful time for me. He cheered up my husband so; his great honest laugh recurs to me; his cheerful company, which drew Frank out of the worries and troubles with his workmen, and restored him to the buoyancy of youth and good fellowship. (I saw him, S. E., a few years ago with such a curious sense of the downfall that time makes — a rather limited person, instead of the genial young man to whom I had always been so grateful for the good cheer he brought into the studio, and the laugh that was so pleasant to hear.) When the idea of a partnership took shape, his brother, Mr (now Sir) John Evans, the well-known antiquary, who was also a business man—paper-maker, one of the 'Times' people—came to go through Frank's books (if he had any books), and see whether it was worth his brother's while. He came afterwards to dine, and it was not till he had gone, after all the long evening, that I heard what the decision was. After Mr Evans had

seen and heard all there was to see and hear, he con-
gratulated my husband that his circumstances permitted
him to be so indifferent to profit. And there was an
end of the partnership, to which I had looked forward
for the sake of the companionship to Frank, I fear not
with much thought of profit. We neither of us, I suppose, knew anything about business—so long as we could
get on and live, that seemed all one cared for; but it
was a little dash as of cold water when the business-
man paid this satirical compliment, and showed us our
true position. I was, of course, writing steadily all the
time, getting about £400 for a novel, and already, of
course, being told that I was working too fast, and
producing too much. I linger upon this brief, and, as
it feels to me now, halcyon time. I used the little back
drawing-room, which was at first dining-room, for my
work, the real dining-room of the house being Frank's
painting-room, where I used to write all the morning,
getting up now and then in the middle of a sentence to
run down-stairs and have a few words with him, or to
play with the children when they came in from their
walk—my dear little Maggie, my baby-boy, two beautiful
children, fresh and sweet, well and strong, reviving my
heart, that had been so heavy and sore with the loss
of my two infants, by the sight of their beautiful shining
faces.

When I look back on my life, among the happy
moments which I can recollect is one which is so
curiously common and homely, with nothing in it, that it
is strange even to record such a recollection, and yet it
embodied more happiness to me than almost any real
occasion as might be supposed for happiness. It was the
moment after dinner when I used to run up-stairs to see
that all was well in the nursery, and then to turn into
my room on my way down again to wash my hands, as
I had a way of doing before I took up my evening
work, which was generally needlework, something to
make for the children. My bedroom had three windows

in it, one looking out upon the gardens I have mentioned, the other two into the road. It was light enough
with the lamplight outside for all I wanted. I can see it
now, the glimmer of the outside lights, the room dark, the
faint reflection in the glasses, and my heart full of joy and
peace—for what?—for nothing—that there was no harm
anywhere, the children well above stairs and their father
below. I had few of the pleasures of society, no gaiety
at all. I was eight-and-twenty, going down-stairs as
light as a feather, to the little frock I was making. My
husband also gone back for an hour or two after dinner
to his work, and well—and the bairnies well. I can feel
now the sensation of that sweet calm and ease and
peace.

I have always said it is in these unconsidered moments
that happiness is—not in things or events that may be
supposed to cause it. How clear it is over these more
than thirty years!

In the early summer one evening after dinner (we
dined, I think, at half-past six in those days) I went
out to buy some dessert-knives on which I had set my
heart—they were only plated, but I had long wanted
them, and by some chance was able to give myself that
gratification. I had marked them in a shop not far off,
and was pleased to get them, and specially happy.
Some one had dined with us, either Sebastian Evans or
my brother-in-law Tom,—some one familiar and intimate
who was with Frank. When I came back again there
was a little agitation, a slight commotion which I could
not understand; and then I was told that it was nothing
—the merest slight matter, nothing to be frightened at.
Frank had, in coughing, brought up a little blood.

And so the happy time came to an end. I don't think
I was much alarmed at first, I knew so little. I was
quite ready to believe, after the first shock, that it might
turn out to be nothing, and to have no consequences.
I was much intent upon going to Scotland that year,
I remember, to Mrs Moir at Musselburgh—and I did go,

Frank promising to join me in a short time. After I was gone I took a great panic in my impulsive way and came in to Edinburgh on Sunday morning and telegraphed to him to know how he was, waiting about the railway station the whole of the Sunday to have an answer, but got none,—only a letter in due time scolding me for my foolishness. We had no habit of telegraphing in those days, it being still a new thing.

But he never was well after. I thought, and perhaps he too thought, that it was the worry of the work, which began to get too much for him, and the difficulty of managing the men, who were of the art-workmen class, and highly paid, and untrustworthy to the last degree. However important it might be to get the work done they were never to be relied upon, not even when they saw him — always most kind and friendly to them, incapable of treating them otherwise than if they had been gentlemen—ill, worn-out, dying by inches; not even when it became a matter of life and death for him to get free. They were well paid, educated in their way, thinking themselves a kind of artists—and I had always been brought up with a high idea of the honour and virtue of working men. I was very indignant at this behaviour, of course, and cruelly undeceived,—and I do not think I have ever got over the impression made upon me by their callousness and want of honour and feeling. I remember most wrathfully contrasting their behaviour with that of my maids, who stood by me to the last moment; knowing we were breaking up our home and going away, and that they would be in no respect advantaged by us, yet who were as loyal and true as the others were selfish and cruel. My husband did not like it to be said—but it was so. Before we decided definitely to give up everything and go abroad, Frank went to consult Dr Walsh, who was the great authority on the lungs at that time. He lived in Harley Street, I think. I went with my husband to the door, and leaving him there walked up and down the street

till he came out again. I think he was to meet Mr
Quain there, who was attending him at the time. And
here again there is a moment that stands out clear
over all these years. I was very anxious, walking up
and down, praying and keeping myself from crying, sick
with anxiety, starting at every sound of a door opening.
He met me with a smile, telling me the report was
excellent. There was very little the matter, chiefly
over - work, and that all would be well when he got
away. The relief was unspeakable : relief from pain is
the highest good on earth, the most exquisite feeling,
—I have always said so. It was in the upper part of
Harley Street that he came up to me and told me this,
and my heart leapt up with this delightful sense of
anxiety stilled.

Afterwards, in Rome, Robert Macpherson told me what
he said was the true story of the consultation—that the
doctors had told Frank his doom ; that his case was
hopeless, but that he had not the courage to tell me
the truth. I was angry and wounded beyond measure,
and would not believe that my Frank had deceived me,
or told another what he did not tell to me. Neither
do I think he would have gone away, to expose me
with my little children to so awful a trial in a foreign
place, had this been the case. And yet the blessed
deliverance of that moment was not real either. The
truth most likely lay between the two.

We left England in January 1859 to go to Italy.
We neither of us knew anything about Italy, but that
it was the sunny South — and of all places in the
world it was Florence we chose to go to in the middle
of winter,—Florence not as it is now, but cold and
austere, without the comforts into which it has been
trained since then. The journey was a dreadful one.
Tom Oliphant went with us to Paris. I have no doubt
that he felt he was taking leave of his brother for the
last time. We were none of us experienced in Con-
tinental travelling, and in those days travellers were

shut up in the waiting-rooms, not allowed to get into
the train till the last moment. It was my first experience of having to take the management of things
myself, and all was new to me, and my French of the
most limited description. Thus it happened that what
with my ignorance, and Tom's leave-taking, and the
two children, and all the excitement and trouble together, our luggage was not registered, nobody thinking
anything about it. We were to sleep at Lyons, and
when we arrived there late at night the luggage was
not forthcoming: we had no ticket,—I knew nothing
about it. Nothing was to be done, accordingly, but to
telegraph to Paris, and remain in Lyons till it came.
We had travelled second-class, one of the few times we
ever did so,—I have always had a stupid objection to
this kind of economy, perhaps to all kinds of economy,
though I have never been extravagant,—so I suppose
our train was a slow one. I remember that there was
a cheerful young fellow in our carriage who belonged
to Beauçain, and who kept Frank amused, and, as it
became cold in the afternoon, took off his own coat to
add to the shawls and rugs that were piled upon him,
and got out at one of the stations to bring a *chauffe-
pied* or *chauffrette*—a thing filled with wood embers—for
his feet: the hot-water stools which are such a nuis-
ance now did not exist then, in second-class at least.
How grateful I was to this young man, and how
warmly I remember his kindness over all these years!
The luggage episode made us very late. We were detained at the cold dark station at Lyons till all the
other passengers were gone, and not a cab was to be
found. At last we were allowed to share one that
passed with a single passenger in it, and so got to our
hotel—a helpless party as ever was. My poor Frank,
ill and worn out, cold and miserable, myself so unaccustomed to manage, good Jane who had never been
in a foreign country before, and the two little ones,
Maggie five, Cyril two—and nothing with us to make

them comfortable, not even a hand-bag, not a night-gown for the children. These little miseries are very bad at the time, but I never was one to make much of them. I remember Lyons, however, as one of the coldest places I ever was in, and the great blank desolation of the immense Place Belcœur, I think. Next day Frank insisted that I should go out to see the place, though he would not leave the house him-self; and I drove, taking Jane and the children with me, to Notre Dame de Fourvières, where there was a wonderful view over the town, and the strange little church full of ex-votos, which I looked at with a be-wildering ignorance, and with such an aching and miserable heart, realising for a moment all the misery of the journey, my inability to do anything for Frank, my utter solitude in this pretence at sight-seeing, which I was doing so against my will in obedience to his whim. I think that in some things I was younger than my years. I was thirty, but with very little ex-perience of the world, and always shy and apt to keep behind backs. I forget if the luggage came that night, but I think it did, and there arose another difficulty. We were but very sparingly supplied with money, and had brought just enough for the journey to Marseilles and one night's rest at Lyons. Circular notes, I think, were scarcely used then,—at all events, what we had was a letter of credit. And next morning I found that we had not enough to pay our bill and journey, and that it was a *fête*, and the banks all closed. This sort of thing has never been a bugbear to me as to many people, and I went to the landlord of the hotel and told him exactly how things were, though with no small trembling. No one, however, could be more kind than he was. He would not even take from me what I could have paid him, but gave me the address of a hotel at Marseilles where he directed me to go, and pay his bill there. We went away, therefore, in much better spirits, having our boxes, and with that

D

elated consciousness of having been kindly treated, which, I suppose, gives one a feeling somehow of having deserved it, of having been appreciated, for it certainly warms the heart and improves the aspect of everything. Frank must have been better, for I remember walking down to the harbour with him when we got to Marseilles, and discovering—with what thankfulness!—that the boat for Leghorn had sailed, and that we must either wait two days for another or go on by land. I hate the sea, and had always longed to do this, but had not, I suppose, liked to propose it, or else had been overruled by my husband. We went on accordingly to Nice by diligence, which was not very comfortable, for we were in the interior, the five of us, with two other people,—a man and his son going to Antibes, where the lad was to draw for the conscription. I forget whether it was on this journey or when we were approaching Marseilles that the sunrise upon the new unaccustomed landscape struck me so — the awful rose of dawn coming over the wide sweep of the country, the mulberry trees all stripped of their leaves, standing out against the growing light. This seems rather a mingling of features; but it is the impression that remains on my mind, and the great silence and the sleeping faces of my companions grey in the rising of the daylight. I remember, too, the delightful sweeps and folds of the Maritime Alps, the green of the cork-trees, as I was told, and the heavenly curves of the coast; and Cannes, which I seem to see as little more than a village, lying half on the hill and half on the beach, with one great stone pine standing up against the extraordinary blue of the sea. How familiar and commonplace later, how wonderful and novel then, like Paradise, the gardens of oranges, the hedges of aloes! We must have been about twenty-four hours in the diligence or more, and got to Nice, I think, in the afternoon. By this time, I suppose, my inclination to careless expenditure (such as it was, so little to anybody that had any margin) must have got the better of Frank's wiser instincts, for we stayed a day or two at Nice, and went the rest of the way in a vettura. So far as I recollect, we stopped only once —at Alassio—between Nice and Genoa. I shall never forget that night : the hotel was an old palace, and in those days comfort had scarcely invaded even those coasts of the Riviera. We were taken into a huge room with a shining marble floor, one or two rugs in front of the fireplace and by the side of the bed, and no fire. The mere sight of the place was enough to freeze the tired traveller, so ill and languid to begin with. I feel still the chill that went into my heart at the sight of this room, so unfit for him ; but we soon got a blazing fire. I remember kneeling by it lighting it with the great fir cones, which blazed up so quickly, and all the reflections, as if in water, in the dark polished marble of the floor.

At Genoa we were somehow strangely fortunate. We went to what I have always supposed to be the Hôtel de la Ville, but that must have been a mistake, and I believe it was the Croce di Malta. It was one of the hotels close to the bay, looking out over the terrace and promenade that surrounds it. And here, again, the outlook being so lovely and rest so desirable, Frank wanted to stay. The landlady was English, and she offered me a beautiful suite of rooms, a great *salon*, commanding the view, with two large bedrooms attached to it. I was enchanted, but in terror for the price—when she said I might have it for eight francs a-day, the whole apartment. Why she was so good I never could tell. I think it was because of my bonnie little Maggie. Whether she had lost a child like her, or whether I only fancied so, I cannot tell. Perhaps the good woman was sorry for us all, and saw, as I did not see, how little chance there was that my husband would ever return. I recollect now the delight of the beautiful room — the walls all frescoed, not very finely perhaps, but yet the mere fact was some-

thing, the bay lying before the windows, and what was
almost as beautiful at the moment—a great fire; not a
few damp logs as we had been having, but a huge fire
of coals and wood, which warmed my invalid through
and through.   I remember the glow of it and the children
playing on the warm carpet, all so perfect a contrast
to the last night's chill and misery, and the feeling
of settling down in that comfort and warmth, though
it was only for two or three days.   My heart always
contrived to rise whenever it had a chance, and I think
Frank was pleased.

We got into Florence in a fog, and again very chill
and tired.   I remember thinking that it might have been
Manchester for anything one saw or felt that was like the
South, and as soon as that was possible left the hotel
there for lodgings in Via Maggio.   In all this our ignorance and want of experience did us great harm.   The
Via Maggio, a deep street of high houses on the other
side of the Arno, was as unfavourable a spot as we could
have chosen, and to make it worse we were on the shady
side of the street.   The recommendation it had was that
the mistress of the house, Madame Gianini, was again an
English, or rather an Irish woman.   We were on the
second floor—a long straggling apartment with some
rooms towards the Piazza Santo Spirito, I think; and
these were sunny, and we ought to have hired them, but
the *salon* was on the other side, and very cold.   I had
not sense to see how bad that must have been for Frank,
but used the rooms as they were arranged in a helpless
way.   I think there was a dreadful time at first,—he
suffering, unable for any exertion, sitting silent, without
even books, till my soul was crushed, not knowing what
to do or how to rouse him.   I had to go on working
all the time, and not very successfully, our whole
income, which was certain for the time, being £20
a-month, which Mr Blackwood had engaged to send me
on the faith of articles.   To think of the whole helpless
family going to Italy, children and maid and all, upon

that alone!—but things were very cheap in Florence then, and I don't think I was at all afraid, nay, the reverse, always inclined to spend. Of course this must have added to Frank's depression, for which I was sometimes inclined to blame him, not knowing how ill he was. He got rheumatism in addition to other troubles; and I have the clearest vision of him sitting close by the little stove in the corner of the room, wrapped up, with a rug upon his knees, and saying nothing, while I sat near the window, trying with less success than ever before to write, and longing for a word, a cheerful look, to disperse a little the heavy atmosphere of trouble. I forget how we came to know a Mr Skottowe, a lame man, who had been an artist, and who came to see us sometimes, to my great thankfulness, for he cheered Frank a little. There was also the Scotch minister, Mr Macdougall, who is still in Florence, and who sent several people to see me, a beautiful Miss M. among the rest, whose distinction was that she refused a duke! and who had dedicated herself to her old father and mother, then very old, and she no longer young,—a very attractive woman, whose sacrifice I grudged dreadfully, though she did not. I might have got into a little society, but had no desire to do so, nor any pleasure in it. I remember Frank going to see the Pitti or Uffizi for the first time, and coming back in a kind of despair: his feeling was not the *anch' io pittore*, but the other far less cheerful sense of what wonders had been done, and how far he was from being able to come within a hundred miles (as he thought) of what he saw. No doubt illness had much to do with this depression, which I, all sanguine and sure that he could do what he would, were he but well, did not sympathise in,—almost, I fear, felt to be a weakness. He recovered his spirits a little after a time, when the winter began to pass away and good weather came. I remember, however, with great and terrible vividness one scene, one day. It was the funeral day of a young Archduchess. I forget who she was: the

wife of one of the Archduke's sons, who had died
away from Florence and was brought home for burial.
Frank, who was sometimes hard on me, as I on him,
insisted that I should go out to see the procession, which
I did most unwillingly all alone.   It must have been very
early in the year, for it was at his worst time.   I walked
as far as the Porta Santa Trinità, I think, and I don't
think I saw any procession.   It was a grey day, the
sky heavy, the Arno running grey under the bridge,
the hills all grey, the air tingling with the tolling of
the bells, and sombre streams of people flowing towards
the gate where the funeral train was to come in; as
sad as any could be, a young woman forlorn, with
nobody to give me even a kind look, and nothing before or about me that was not as grey and tragic as
the skies.   I paused a little there, having been carried
so far by the instinct of pleasing him who had sent
me out to see; and then I could bear it no longer and
went back again, to find him sitting silent as before
—by the fire.

But things brightened, as I have said, when the
weather improved and it began to get warm.   He
thought of a picture to paint, a scene in which Macchia-
velli should be the chief figure, and we began to visit
the galleries, and to go out together.   All sorts of strange
things—not strange at all now, but wonderful then—
went on in Via Maggio.   Scarcely a night passed but
we heard the chant of a passing funeral, and going to
the window saw far below, as in a deep gorge, the torches
glowing, the strange figures of the *confraternità* carrying
the bier, and their tramp on the stony causeway.   Sometimes it was the *misericordia*, carrying not the dead but
somebody hurt by an accident; and in the daytime the
deep street underneath was always a diversion, and I
used to look out for the dearest sight of all—two little
figures at the feet of tall Jane, or rather the one dear
figure at her feet, the other always with a song or
shout, in her arm against her ample shoulder.   She was

always very big, at this time about four - and - twenty, a finely developed, strong, large, substantial tower of a woman—the ox-eyed Juno, as we used to call her. Ah me! would they come down from the Boboli gardens with their hands full of anemones if I were at the windows of the Casa Grassini now?

While we were there the revolution occurred—which, so much as we saw of it, was more like a popular *festa* than anything else. We had not known, being strangers and Frank so ill, going out little, what was going on; but a curious agitation and excitement made itself some-how felt in the air even up in our second floor. I don't know really except by a sort of sympathetic instinct what it was that took us to the windows to watch the unusual coming and going. And then suddenly opposite us, in the Casa Ridolfi, I think, there was unfurled a great Italian tricolour—the green, white, and red—and in a moment like fire the whole population seemed to blaze out in the national colours, man, woman, child, and horse, every living thing; and there began to be a shout of "Viva l'Italia!" everywhere, wherever two people met in the deep streets, a shout that my dear baby boy took up in that little voice of his that was never silent. I was very eager too; but Frank was rather nervous, and unwilling to be in any way mixed up in the crowd, with whose doings we, as strangers, he thought, had nothing to do. I got him, however, at last to come out, and we went up to the front of the Pitti Palace, where a great many people were hanging about, and where at that moment the Grand Duke was in full colloquy with the representatives of the people. Notwithstanding the excitement of which I was full, it was a little forlorn to stand out there with our very faint knowledge of Italian, and nobody to tell us what was going on; and Frank had no desire to be in the heart of the revolution, if it was a revolution, as I had. Where all the cockades, the rosettes, the rib-bons, the little bouquets, all the red, white, and green

came from, at a moment's notice, or without even
a moment's notice, was an endless wonder to me;
and the delight of the people, and the air of universal
holiday, had none of the graver features that one
expected. I am not sure that I was not a little
disappointed at the entire peacefulness of the whole
proceeding. We heard afterwards that the Grand Duke
had given orders for the bombardment of the town, which
would have had a fine effect indeed in Via Maggio had
it taken place, but I don't know that the report was true.
Florence was at this time the very cheapest place to live
in I have ever known. We had, like most other strangers,
our dinner sent in from the Trattoria every evening. It
was the usual sort of meal—soup, two kinds of meat, one
of them generally a chicken, a vegetable dish, and a
dolce; plenty for us all, with fragments left over, and
the price was five pauls, not quite two francs fifty cen-
times. I wonder if anywhere in Europe that could be
had now.'

We had brought an introduction to the Embassy, and
the Embassy sent us huge cards in return, but took no
more notice, which was just as well: what disappointed
me more was, that the Brownings, to whom also we had
letters, had left Florence for Rome, where we saw them
subsequently. By this time I must have written, I suppose, some half-dozen books or more, and had a little
bit of reputation, a very little bit in a small way, but
was very anxious it should be kept to ourselves. Just
before we left Florence, I remember Mr Skottowe came
one day quite excited; he had heard this from Mr Macdougall, who had heard it accidentally from some one
else. "I thought," he said, "I had found out there
was something out of the common for myself, and now
it appears all the world knows." I wonder if I should
have remembered that, if it had not been a compliment.
I did not get many sweetmeats of the kind, so I suppose
it was a little pleasure to me. I do not know that
Florence itself impressed me very much: how should

it, with my mind so full of other things? — my sick
husband, my little children, my work, and the pre-
cariousness of our means of living (though I don't think
that troubled me much). I remember nature — as I
always do — more than art, and the view from Bellos-
guardo above all the treasures of the galleries. Frank
was profoundly, depressingly, as I have said, impressed
by the pictures at first—and all the glory of them. I
for my part used to stray into one small room in the
Pitti, I think, where at that time the great picture of
the Visitation — Albertinelli's — hung alone. By that
time I knew that another baby was coming, and it
seemed to do me good to go and look at these two
women, the tender old Elizabeth, and Mary with all
the awe of her coming motherhood upon her. I had
little thought of all that was to happen to me before
my child came, but I had no woman to go to, to be
comforted—except these two.

Florence was just becoming warm and bright and good
for an invalid to live in, when Frank was seized with a
desire to go to Rome. I think he had heard from Robert
Macpherson, to whom he was attached. I had only seen
him once in London, and he was too noisy, too much
unlike anything I knew, to please me. And I was very
much afraid for the children. It was just the time when
people are leaving, not going to, Rome ; and one heard
of malaria and fever and all sorts of dreadful things.
But Frank had set his heart upon it, and there was
nothing more to be said. I think it very likely that, feeling himself no better, and having the doctor's verdict,
which he had not told me, in his mind, he wanted me to
be near the Macphersons, who would be a help and stand
by. We went on accordingly to Rome in May. I had
not been very successful in my work for ' Blackwood.'
I sent a story of Florence called ' Felicita,' I think
(knowing nothing about Florence !), and other articles,
not good, and I suppose I must have written something
for Mr Blackett while in Florence, but I cannot recollect.

We could not certainly have struck our tents as we did
and moved on to Rome, by steamboat from Leghorn to
Civita Vecchia, on our twenty pounds a-month. I remember all about the journey strangely enough, from the
green water, so translucent and profound under the boat,
that took us out to the steamer at Leghorn, and the
remarks of some Irish ladies, who were the companions
of the voyage, and who made friends with the children,
and suggested, perhaps guessing from some sad look in
my face, that there had been some loss between the two,
—there were but three years between them, but there
had been two babies born to die : I don't remember their
names nor anything about them except that, and that
they were kind—and Irish. Half of the people I have
met travelling have always been Irish. Maggie was five
and a half, with her brown curls falling on her shoulders,
and my little Cyril was two and a half; always the
sweetest, most winning child.   He had been called
Cyril at first, then by himself when he began to talk
Tiddy, which was always his family name all his life,
though not a pretty one; sometimes Tids, which is
almost too dear, too familiar and tender, the most caressing of all, to be thought of now.   But I must not begin
to write of my boy, or I will not be able to think of anything else—not five months yet since he has been taken
from me !

The Macphersons had a curious position in Rome,
and it is difficult to describe them. He always had a
curious position,—the son of a very poor man in Edinburgh with the humblest connections, yet not distantly
related, I believe, to Cluny Macpherson, the chief of the
clan; himself a poor painter—literally a poor painter,
never good for very much, yet always, as I have been
told, in society, and with friends quite beyond his apparent position. There was some romantic story about
a lady in the Highlands, intercepted letters and so forth,
which was told on one side as the reason for his leaving
the country with something like a broken heart, but on

the other was made to appear like the disappointment of a fortune-hunter. I don't know which was true. There was very little that was like a fortune-hunter in his careless, hot-headed, humorous, noisy Bohemian ways. He had given up his painting in Rome, and had taken to photographing; and his photographs of Rome were, I think, among the first that were executed. He had been a long time in Rome, had been there during the bombardment, and I suppose had rendered some services to the papal side, for he was always patronised more or less by the priests, and was *nero* to the heart, standing by all the old institutions with the stout prejudices of an old Tory quite inaccessible to reason. Indeed reason had nothing to do with him. He was full of generosities and kindness, full of humour and whim and fun — quarrelling hotly and making up again; a big, bearded, vehement, noisy man, a combination of Highlander and Lowlander, Scotsman and Italian, with the habits of Rome and Edinburgh all rubbed together, and a great knowledge of the world in general and a large acquaintance with individuals in particular to give force to the mixture, and to increase his own interest and largeness as a man. I could not bear him at first, poor Robert,—we used to quarrel upon almost every subject; but in the end I got to be almost fond of him, as he was, I believe, of me, though we were so absolutely unlike. Some years before I was married he had married Geraldine Bate, a niece of Mrs Jameson, very much against the aunt's will, to whom the Roman photographer seemed a very poor match for her pretty Geddie at eighteen. And so he was, and it was not a very successful marriage, chiefly perhaps, notwithstanding my indignation with the popular fallacy about mothers-in-law, because of the constant presence in their house of Mrs Bate, who, though entirely maintained by his bounty, constantly encouraged Geddie in her little rebellions against her husband and her love of gaiety and admiration. But Robert was no meek victim, and never hesitated to tell mamma his mind. There used to be a

fierce row often in the house, from which he would stride
forth plucking his red beard and sending forth fire and
flame; but when he came back would have his hands full
of offerings, even to the mother-in-law, and his face full
of sunshine, as if it had never known a cloud. Geddie
was of course full of faults, untidy, disorderly, fond of
gaiety of every kind, incapable of the dull domestic life
which seemed the right thing to me, ready to go off upon
a merrymaking at a moment's notice, indifferent what
duty she left behind, yet quite as ready to give up night
after night to nurse a sick friend, and to put herself to
any inconvenience to help, or take entirely upon her
shoulders, those who were in need. And though full
of natural indolence, working like a slave—nay, as no
slave ever worked—at the common trade, the photographing, at which she did quite as much as, if not, people
said, more than, he did. And a pretty creature, and full
of vivacity and wit, a delightful companion. A strange
house it was, a continual coming and going of artists and
patrons of artists; of Scottish visitors, of Italian great
personages and priests, and more or less of all the
English in Rome. They were, I think, in one of their
best times (for they had many vicissitudes) when we
went to Rome first in 1859—and saw everybody.

My husband was much revived at first by the change
and by the company of Robert, to whom he had a
faithful and long attachment from his boyish days, and
we went with them to their *villeggiatura* at Nettuno
in May. It is now, I believe, a sea-bathing place, well
enough known; but then it was the rudest Italian village,
one of the most curious places I have ever seen. I
described it in a little sketch I made for 'Blackwood,'
calling it a seaside place in the Papal States, or some
such title. The rooms, the living, everything was in-
conceivably rough, the place like a great medieval
fortress upon the rocks, with the natural agglomeration
of houses hanging about its skirts. The women were
handsome and wore a beautiful dress, red satin in long

box-plaits, Greek jackets embroidered with gold, and beautiful embroidered white aprons and kerchiefs, with a very pretty half-Eastern headdress. We had some very bad and some good days there. Very bad at first, and I very miserable; but later Frank took to working, and made one very pretty picture of a group of lads from the country, whom he saw and brought into the loggia to stand to him. It hangs in my drawing-room now. He also made two sketches of the place itself, which are in my own room, his last work. This must have meant that he was feeling better. But I remember some dreadful scenes in the middle of the night, when his nose-bleeding came on, and I stood by him for hours, holding the nostril till the blood dried, he going to sleep in the meantime, while I stood with the traces all about as if I were murdering him. I remember one time when they all went off along the coast to Astura, the Macphersons and Frank with them, leaving me alone with the children,—probably my own fault, as I always had a foolish proud way of holding back,—and how I got over my little disappointment, and did my very best to get a good dinner for them to come back to, and arranged everything as nicely as possible, yet when they did come, could not keep it up, and was sulky, and injured, and disagreeable, notwithstanding that I had really taken a great deal of trouble to have everything ready and pleasant for the party. What trifles remain in one's mind! I suppose it was because I contrived to be half sorry for myself, and half ashamed of myself, that I remember this so clearly.

When we left Nettuno we went to Frascati, where we lived for more than three months, I think, and which at first was very pleasant with its great prospect over the misty Campagna, where St Peter's was visible, the only sign of the existence of Rome. We used to go out and walk on the terrace from whence there was that view, — and sometimes had a little society, the

Noccioli, and Monsignor Pentini, afterwards Cardinal—
an old trooper priest, who had been a soldier in Ber-
nadotte's army, and then was supposed too liberal for
promotion, having been kept back a long time from
the Cardinal's hat he ought to have had. He was very
kind, very benignant, the providence and at the same
time the judge of all the poor people round, whom he
kept from litigation, settling all their quarrels. I remember once or twice supping with him and good Ser
Antonio, and his fat big Irish wife,—such good simple
people, Monsignor not able to talk to me, nor I to
him, though he gave me many a kind look. I understood pretty well what he said, but could not express
myself either in French or Italian. The Noccioli lived
in the upper floor of his big old square house, with a
wonderful view from the windows, and partially frescoed walls, scarcely any furniture, and a supper-table
gleaming under the three clear flames of the Roman
lamp, and the melons on the table, which Monsignor
ate, I remember, with pepper and salt. But Frank
grew very ill here. He became altogether unable to
eat anything, not comparatively but absolutely; and
the awful sensation of watching this, trying with every
faculty to find something he could eat, and always fail-
ing, makes me shiver even now, though, God help me!
I have had almost a repetition of it. We got an
Italian doctor there, who was quite cheerful, as I believe is their way when nothing can be done, and spoke
of our return next year, which gave me a little confidence. On the 1st of October we went back to
Rome, to an apartment we had got in the Noccioli's
house in the Babuino, where he got worse and worse.
We had Dr Small, who brought a famous French doctor, and they told me there was no hope : it was better
to tell me *franchement,* the Frenchman said, and that
word *franchement* always, even now, gives me a thrill
when I read it. They told me, or I imagined they
told me in my confused state, that they had told

him, and I went back to him not trying to command
my tears; but found they had not told him, and that
it was I in my misery who was taking him the news.
I remember he said after a while, "Well, if it is so,
that is no reason why we should be miserable." In
my condition of health I was terrified that I might
be disabled from attending my Frank to the last.
Whether I took myself, or the doctor gave me, a dose
of laudanum, I don't remember; but I recollect very
well the sudden floating into ease of body and the dazed
condition of mind,—a kind of exaltation, as if I were
walking upon air, for I could not sleep in the circumstances nor try to sleep. I thought then that this was
the saving of me. I nursed my husband night and
day, neither resting nor eating, sometimes swallowing
a sandwich when I came out of his room for a moment, sometimes dozing for a little when he slept—
reading to him often in the middle of the night to try
to get him to sleep. And when I came out of the room
and sat down in the next and got the relief of crying
a little, my bonnie boy came up and stood at my knee
and pulled down my head to him, and smiled all
over his beaming little face,—smiled though the child
wanted to cry too, but would not — not quite three
years old. When his father was dead I remember
him sitting in his bed in the next room singing "Oh
that will be joyful, when we meet to part no more,"
which was the favourite child's hymn of the moment.
Frank died quite conscious, kissing me when his lips
were already cold, and quite, quite free from anxiety,
though he left me with two helpless children and one
unborn, and very little money, and no friends but the
Macphersons, who were as good to me as brother and
sister; but had no power to help beyond that, if anything could be beyond that. Everybody was very kind.
Mr Blackett wrote offering to come out to me, to bring
me home; and John Blackwood wrote bidding me draw
upon him for whatever money I wanted. I had sent

for Effie M., my husband's niece, to come out to me,
sending money for her journey; but her mother arrived
some time after Frank's death, his sister, Mrs Murdoch
—a kind but useless woman, who was no good to me,
and yet was a great deal of good as a sort of background and backbone to our helpless little party,—for
I was young still, thirty-one, and never self-confident.
And there we waited six weeks till my baby was born—
he as fair and sweet and healthful as if everything had
been well with us.   My big Jane was my stand - by,
and took the child from the funny Italian-Irish nurse,
Madame Margherita, who attended and cheered me with
her jolly ways, and brought me back, she and the baby
together, to life.   By degrees, so wonderful are human
things, there came to be a degree of comfort, even
cheerfulness; the children being always bright,—Maggie
and Cyril the sweetest pair, and my bonnie rosy baby.
While I write, October 5, 1894, he, the last, is lying
in his coffin in the room next to me — I have been
trying to pray by the side of that last bed — and he
looks more beautiful than ever he did in his life, in
a sort of noble manhood, like, so very like, my infant
of nearly thirty-five years ago.   All gone, all gone, and
no light to come to this sorrow any more!   When my
Cecco was two months old we came home—Mrs Murdoch and Jane and the three children and I—travelling
expensively as was my way, though heaven knows our
position was poor enough.

      When I thus began the world anew I had for all
my fortune about £1000 of debt, a small insurance of,
I think, £200 on Frank's life, our furniture laid up in
a warehouse, and my own faculties, such as they were,
to make our living and pay off our burdens by.

                              Christmas Night, 1894.
      I feel that I must try to change the tone of this record.
It was written for my boys, for Cecco in particular.
Now they will never see it — unless, indeed, they are

permitted, being in a better place, to know what is going on here. I used to feel that Cecco would use his discretion,—that most likely he would not print any of this at all, for he did not like publicity, and would have thought his mother's story of her life sacred; but now everything is changed, and I am now going to try to remember more trivial things, the incidents that sometimes amuse me when I look back upon them, not merely the thread of my life.

Robert Macpherson came down with us to Civita Vecchia to see us off, and, I remember, read to me all the way there a story he had written, one of the stories flying about Rome of one of the great families, which he wanted me to polish up and get published for him. It was very bad, poor dear fellow, and beyond doing anything with. I used another of these stories which he told me, in a little thing I did for 'Blackwood' some time later, the strange tale of the Cæsarini — but that was too bad. Robert introduced me to Dr Kennedy of Shrewsbury when we got on board the steamer,—a large, loose-lipped, loquacious man, full of talk, whom I liked well enough, and who talked to me pleasantly enough. He had two or three young men with him. I have always had a half-amused grudge against him, however. We were a very helpless party, the baby two months old and three other children, for I was bringing Willie Macpherson home to his aunt. In those days we had to land at Marseilles by small boats, which crowded round the steamer as soon as she came to anchor, and waited till the passengers had shown their passports and got through all the preliminaries. I saw that Dr Kennedy had engaged a large boat, and, though he said nothing to me, I was so foolish as to take it for granted that he meant me and my helpless party to go to the shore with him. It amuses me to think how astonished, how wounded and indignant I was, when, getting through before me, he and his young men stepped into their boat without a word, and left me to get ashore as I could

E

—which, of course, I did all right, never having had
any difficulty in that way of taking care of myself and
my own belongings. I dare say he was quite right,
and I had no claim upon him whatever,—and he was a
good man, no doubt, and a great scholar. But it could
not have hurt him to have helped a young woman and
her children. I was so much astonished that I could
scarcely believe my eyes. I remember that same night
at the railway station, when we were all getting off by
the *rapide*, I haughtily desired one of the young men
to stand by two of the children while I got them all
into a compartment, which he did meekly and rather
frightened. I did not know where to go in Paris, as
I could not go back to the same hotel where we had
been when my husband was with me; and in our
innocence we went to the Bristol!—my sister-in-law
having been advised to go there, at second or third hand,
through Mr Pentland. The rooms were delightful, but
so were the prices, which I inquired, as we had been
taught to do in Italy, before taking possession. I
faltered, and said we had been sent there by Mr Pentland—but—— The name acted like magic. Mr Pentland, ah! that was another thing,—the rooms were just
half the price to a friend of Mr Pentland. He was
the editor of Murray's Handbooks — but of that important fact I was not aware.

We arrived late at night in London, having been
detained at Calais by a storm, and got in with the
greatest difficulty to the Paddington Hotel.

After this we passed some time with my brother's
family at Birkenhead, which was not very successful.
I think it was rather more than I could bear to see
his children rushing to the door to meet him when he
came home, and my fatherless little ones ready to rush
too, though it was so short a time since their father
had been taken from them. I was always fantastical—
and there were other things. It is a perilous business
when one is very sorry for oneself, and the sight of

happy people is apt, when one's wounds are fresh, to make the consciousness keener.

I was reading of Charlotte Brontë the other day, and could not help comparing myself with the picture more or less as I read. I don't suppose my powers are equal to hers — my work to myself looks perfectly pale and colourless beside hers — but yet I have had far more experience and, I think, a fuller conception of life. I have learned to take perhaps more a man's view of mortal affairs,—to feel that the love between men and women, the marrying and giving in marriage, occupy in fact so small a portion of either existence or thought. When I die I know what people will say of me: they will give me credit for courage (which I almost think is not courage but insensibility), and for honesty and honourable dealing; they will say I did my duty with a kind of steadiness, not knowing how I have rebelled and groaned under the rod. Scarcely anybody who cares to speculate further will know what to say of my working power and my own conception of it; for, except one or two, even my friends will scarcely believe how little possessed I am with any thought of it all,—how little credit I feel due to me, how accidental most things have been, and how entirely a matter of daily labour, congenial work, sometimes now and then the expression of my own heart, almost always the work most pleasant to me, this has been. I wonder if God were to try me with the loss of this gift, such as it is, whether I should feel it much? If I could live otherwise I do not think I should. If I could move about the house, and serve my children with my own hands, I know I should be happier. But this is vain talking; only I know very well that for years past neither praise nor blame has quickened my pulse ten beats that I am aware of. This insensibility saves me some pain, but it must also lose me a great deal of pleasure.

III.

I RESUME this from the old book which contains my recollections up to 1859, when I came home from Rome with my three children, Cecco a baby of two months old. I stayed for some months, as I have said, with my brother in Birkenhead, and then went to Scotland—to Fife — for the summer, taking a small house in Elie. The Milligans (Mrs Milligan was Anne Mary Moir, a daughter of Delta, one of the girl friends whom I liked to have to stay with me in the early days of my married life in London) were at Kilconquhar, where Mr Milligan was minister, a man afterwards distinguished in his way, a well-known Biblical scholar and professor at Aberdeen. I was still only thirty-one, and in full convalescence of sorrow, and feeling myself unaccountably young notwithstanding my burdened life and my widow's cap, which, by the way, I put off a year or two afterwards for the curious reason that I found it too becoming! That did not seem to me at all suitable for the spirit of my mourning : it certainly was, as my excellent London dressmaker made it for me, a very pretty head-dress, and an expensive luxury withal.

The Blackwoods were at Gibleston for the summer, a place quite near, so that I had friends within reach. I had not seen very much of John Blackwood, but he was already a friend, with that curious kind of intimacy which is created by a publisher's knowledge of all one's affairs, especially when these affairs mean struggles to keep afloat and a constant need of money. He had bidden me draw upon him when my husband died, and I was very grateful and apt to boast of it, as I have or had a way of doing; so that people who have served me in this way, even when, as sometimes happened, the balance changed a little, have always conceived themselves to be my benefactors. But he was a genial benefactor, and he and his wife used to come to see me; so that, though lonely and a stranger, I was not entirely out of a kind of society. I must, however, have been very lonely, except for the sweet company of my three little children and my good Jane, my factotum, who had gone with me to Rome as their nurse, and helped me in my trouble, and stood faithfully by me through all. I always remember, immediately after we came home, one dreadful night when my dear baby was very ill, and was laid upon her capacious shoulder as on a feather-bed, while I watched in anguish, thinking the night would never be done or that he would not live through it, when suddenly, with one of those rapid turns peculiar to infants, he got almost well in a moment! And this picture got itself hung up upon the walls of my mind, full of a roseate glow of happiness and deliverance instead of the black despair which had seemed to be closing round me.

That winter we went to Edinburgh, where I got a droll little house in Fettes Row, down at the bottom of the hill, the lower floor and the basement with a front door, in truly Edinburgh style—for "flats" were not known in England in those days. It was a very severe winter, 1860-61, and it was severe on me too. I have told the story of one incident in it in my other book, but I may repeat it here. I had not been doing very well with my writing. I had sent several articles, though of what nature I don't remember, to 'Blackwood,' and they had been rejected. Why, this being the case, I should have gone to them (John Blackwood and the Major were the firm at that moment) to offer them, or rather to suggest to them that they should take a novel

from me for serial publication, I can't tell,—they so
jealous of the Magazine, and inclined to think nothing
was good enough for it, and I just then so little successful. But I was in their debt, and had very little to go
on with. They shook their heads of course, and thought
it would not be possible to take such a story,—both very
kind and truly sorry for me, I have no doubt. I think
I see their figures now against the light, standing up,
John with his shoulders hunched up, the Major with
his soldierly air, and myself all blackness and whiteness
in my widow's dress, taking leave of them as if it didn't
matter, and oh! so much afraid that they would see the
tears in my eyes. I went home to my little ones, running
to the door to meet me with "flichterin' noise and glee";
and that night, as soon as I had got them all to bed,
I sat down and wrote a story which I think was something about a lawyer, John Brownlow, and which formed
the first of the Carlingford series,—a series pretty well
forgotten now, which made a considerable stir at the
time, and *almost* made me one of the popularities of
literature. *Almost*, never quite, though 'Salem Chapel'
really went very near it, I believe. I sat up nearly all
night in a passion of composition, stirred to the very
bottom of my mind. The story was successful, and my
fortune, comparatively speaking, was made. It has never
been very much, never anything like what many of my
contemporaries attained, and yet I have done very well
for a woman, and a friendless woman with no one to
make the best of me, and quite unable to do that for
myself. I never could fight for a higher price or do
anything but trust to the honour of those I had to
deal with. Whether this was the reason why, though
I did very well on the whole, I never did anything like
so well as others, I can't tell, or whether it was really
inferiority on my part. Anthony Trollope must have
made at least three times as much as ever I did, and
even Miss Muloch. As for such fabulous successes as
that of Mrs Humphry Ward, which we poorer writers

are all so whimsically and so ruefully unable to explain, nobody thought of them in these days.

I did not see many people in Edinburgh. I was still in deep mourning, and shy, and not clever about society — constantly forgetting to return calls, and avoiding invitations. I met a few people at the Blackwoods', and I remember in the dearth of incidents an amusing evening (which I think, however, came a few years later) when Professor Aytoun dined at Miss Blackwood's, he and I being the only guests. Miss Blackwood was one of the elders of the Blackwood family, and at this period a comely, black-haired, dark-complexioned person, large, and much occupied with her dress, and full of amusing peculiarities, with a genuine drollery and sense of fun, in which all the family were strong. She was sometimes the most intolerable person that could be conceived, and insulted her friends without compunction; but the effect upon me at least was always this — that before the end of one of her tirades she would strike, half consciously, a comical note, and my exasperation would explode into laughter. She was full of recollections of all sorts of people, and of her own youthful successes, which, though stout and elderly, she never outgrew,— still remembering the days when she was called a sylph, and never quite sure that she was not making a triumphant impression even in these changed circumstances. She was very fond of conversation, and truly exceedingly queer in the remarks she would make, sometimes so totally out of all sequence that the absurdity had as good an effect as wit, and often truly droll and amusing, after the fashion of her family. I remember when some people were discussing the respective merits of Rome and Florence, Miss Blackwood gave her vote for Rome. "Ah," she said with an ecstatic look, "when you have read the 'Iliad' in your youth, it all comes back!" Another favourite story of her was, that when one of her brothers asked her, on mischief bent, no doubt, "Isabella, what are filbert nails?" she held out

her hand towards him, where he was sitting a little
behind her, without a word. She had a beautiful hand,
and was proud of it.

But I have not told my story of Aytoun. Miss
Blackwood had asked him to dine with us alone, and
he came, and we flattered him to the top of his bent,
she half sincerely, with that quaint mixture of enthusiasm
and ridicule which I used to say was the Blackwood
attitude towards that droll, partly absurd, yet more or
less effective thing called an author; and I, I fear,
backing her up in pure fun, for I was no particular
admirer of Aytoun, who was then an ugly man in middle
age, with the air of being one of the old lights, but
without either warmth or radiancy. We got him
between us to the pitch of flattered fatuity which all
women recognise, when a man looks like the famous
scene painter, "I am so sick, I am so clevare"; his
eyes bemused and his features blunted with a sort of
bewildered beatitude, till suddenly he burst forth without
any warning with "Come hither, Evan Cameron"—and
repeated the poem to us, Miss Blackwood, ecstatic,
keeping a sort of time with flourishes of her hand, and
I, I am afraid, overwhelmed with secret laughter. I am
not sure that he did not come to himself with a horrified
sense of imbecility before he reached the end.

I got rather intimate with old Mrs Wilson, a very
dear old lady, the mother of my sister-in-law, Jeanie,
and of Dr George Wilson and Sir Daniel Wilson—who
lived at quite a great distance from me, a very long walk
which I used to take every Sunday afternoon, with a
complacent sense that it was a fine thing to do. She had
a lonely day on Sunday, being very deaf, and unable to go
to church, and her daughter much occupied by Sunday
classes, &c. Although deaf, she was an amusing and
good talker, and used to give me all sorts of good advice,
and tell me stories of her life. Her advice was chiefly
about my children, whom she wished me to bring up
on Museums and the broken bread of Science, which

I loathed, pointing out to me with triumph how this system had succeeded with her own sons. It was a very long walk to Elm Cottage. I don't know Edinburgh well enough to say exactly where it was, but I had to mount the hill to Princes Street, and then go somehow by Bruntsfield Links, I think, past a Roman Catholic Convent (St Margaret's?), and a long solitary way beyond that. I was rather proud of myself for resisting all temptations to take a cab, though the dark road by the Nunnery, which was very lonely, used to frighten me considerably.

It was then I first became acquainted with the Storys, Mr, afterwards Dr, Story coming to see me in respect to my proposed Memoir of Edward Irving, which he had by some means heard about. My article in 'Blackwood' on Irving must have been published that winter: no, no, it was published much before we went to Italy, and I had been to Albury to see Mr Drummond,[1] my husband accompany-

---

[1] Mr Drummond wrote to me when the article on Irving, which was in a manner the germ of the book, was published. It must have been in the end of 1848. He and all his community were much pleased with it, and had a notion, which my Roman Catholic friends always share, that since I went so far with them I must go the whole way. They gave me great encouragement accordingly, and I was supposed to be going to do just what they wanted to have done. We went to Albury on Mr Drummond's invitation, where we stayed three days, I think ; and I remember the sensation with which I sat and listened while Mr Drummond, the caustic wit and man of the world, explained to me how they were guided in setting up their church, and in building their quasi-cathedral in Gordon Square, and of the pillars called Jachin and Boaz, and a great deal more, while Lord Lovaine, his son-in-law, now Duke of Northumberland,[*] a grave man, whose aspect impressed me much, listened gravely, as if to an oracle, and I looked on and wondered, amazed, as I sometimes used to be when Montalembert, at the combination of what seems to my hard head so much nonsense with so much keen sense and power ; though I had much more sympathy with Montalembert, even with his medieval miracles, than with Jachin and Boaz. These good people thought, partly because of their deep sense of their own importance, and partly by a trick of sympathy which I had, and most genuine it was, that I was interested beyond measure in them and their ways, whereas it was in Irving I was interested, and listening with all my ears to hear about him, and much less concerned about the Holy Apostolic Church. They were disappointed accordingly, and not pleased with the book.

---

[*] Died January 1899.

ing me, which was the first beginning of that project.
Mr Story told me of his father's long intimacy with
Irving, and promised me many letters if I would go to
the manse of Roseneath to see them. I went accordingly,
rather unwillingly in cold February weather, grudging the
absence from my children for a few days very much. I
did not know anything about the West of Scotland, and,
winter as it was, the lovely little loch was a revelation
to me, with the wonderful line of hills called the Duke's
Bowling Green, which I afterwards came to know so
well. The family at the manse was a very interesting
one. The handsome young minister, quite young, though
already beginning to grow grey—a very piquant combination (I was so myself, though older by several years than
he)—and his mother, a handsome old lady full of strong
character, and then a handsome sister with her baby,
the most interesting of all, with a shade of mystery about
her. They were, as people say, like a household in a
novel, and attracted my curiosity very much. But when
I was sent to my room with a huge packet of letters, and
the family all retired for the night, and the deep darkness
and silence of a winter night in the country closed down
upon me, things were less delightful. The bed in my
room was a gloomy creation, with dark-red moreen cur-
tains, afterwards, as I found, called by Mr Story—witty
and profane—" a field to bury strangers in." I had a pair
of candles, which burned out, and a fire, which got low,
while I agonised over the letters, not one of which I
could make out. The despairing puzzle of that diabolical
handwriting, which was not Irving's after all (who wrote
a beautiful hand), but only letters addressed to him, and
the chill that grew upon me, and the gradual sense of
utter stupidity that came over me, I can't attempt to
describe. I sat up half the night, but in vain. Next
day Mr Campbell of Row came specially to see me, a
little shocked, I am afraid, to find the future biographer
of Irving a young person, rather apt to be led astray and
laugh with the young people in the midst of his serious

talk. Mr Campbell had been a very notable character in these parts, and was at that time reverenced and admired as an apostle, though perhaps to me a little too much disposed, like everybody else, to tell me of himself instead of telling me of Irving, on whom my soul was bent. I never have had, I fear, a strong theological turn, and his exposition at family prayers, though I did my best to think it very interesting, confounded me, especially next morning when I had to catch the boat at a certain hour in order to catch the train and get home to my babies. All these details, however, gave a whimsical mixture of fun, to which, a sort of convalescent as I was from such trouble and sorrow, and long deprived of cheerful society, my mind yielded, in spite of a little resistance on the part of my graver side, which had honestly expected never to laugh again. This visit laid the foundation of a long friendship and much and generally very lively intercourse.

How strange it is to me to write all this, with the effort of making light reading of it, and putting in anecdotes that will do to quote in the papers and make the book sell! It is a sober narrative enough, heaven knows! and when I wrote it for my Cecco to read it was all very different, but now that I am doing it consciously for the public, with the aim (no evil aim) of leaving a little more money, I feel all this to be so vulgar, so common, so unnecessary, as if I were making pennyworths of myself. Well! what does it matter? Will my boys ever see it? Do they ever see me? Have they the power, as some one says, of being present when they desire to be by a mere process of thought? I would rather it were not so. I should not like to fix them to earth, to an old mother, an old woman, when they are both young men in the very height of life. But why should I turn back here to this continual strain of my thoughts? There is too much of this already. I got a letter from Dr Story

the other day, from Taymouth, about which we had
wandered once together in a little holiday expedition
full of talk and frolic, more than thirty years ago. It
was a very kind letter. I could see that his heart
swelled with pity for the lonely woman, bereaved of
all things, whom he had known so different. Good
friend, though we have drifted so far apart since then.
But I must try to begin again.

I saw various other people besides Mr Campbell and
the Storys, in pursuit of information about Irving, and
came across some amusing scenes, though they have
passed out of my recollection for the most part. I remember making the discovery already noted—which, of
course, I promulgated to all my friends—that every one
I saw on this subject displayed the utmost willingness
to tell me all about themselves, with quite a secondary
interest in Irving. One gentleman in Edinburgh told
me the whole story of his own wife's illness and death,
and that he had reflected on the evening of her death
that his children were almost more to be pitied than
himself, since it was possible that he might get a new
wife, while they could never have a new mother. Not
an original thought, perhaps, but curious as occurring
at such a moment. This was told me *apropos* of the
fact that Irving, I think, had once dined in the house
during the reign of that poor lady. She had more
than one successor, if I remember rightly.

One of my people whom I went to see on this subject
was Dr Carlyle, whom I found surrounded with huge
books, — books of a kind with which I was afterwards well acquainted—the 'Acta Sanctorum' and the
like. He was writing a life of Adamnan, the successor
of Columba. My recollection of him is of a small, rather
spruce man, not at all like his great brother. (Mrs Carlyle used to say of Dr John that he was one of the people
who seemed to have been born in creaking shoes.) It
must have been he who told me to go and see Carlyle

himself, who could tell me a great deal more than he could about Irving. I fancy that I must have made a run up to London from Edinburgh in the summer of 1861, and stayed with Mrs Powell in Palace Gardens— a sister of Mr Maurice, who had been very kind and friendly to me for a year or two before my husband's death. This must have been my first visit to her after, for I remember that she questioned me as to how I was "left," and that I answered her cheerfully, "With my head and my hands to provide for my children," and was truly surprised by her strange look and dumb amazement at my cheerfulness. I suppose now, but never thought then, that it was something to be amazed at. I don't remember that I ever thought it anything the least out of the way, or was either discouraged or frightened, provided only that the children were all well.

It was on this occasion that, shy as I always was, yet with the courage that comes to one when one is about one's lawful work, and not seeking acquaintance or social favour, I bearded the lion in his den, and went to see Mr Carlyle in the old house in Cheyne Row, which people are now trying, I think very unwisely, to make a shrine or museum of, which I should myself hate to see. He received me (I suppose I must have had an introduction from his brother) with that perfect courtesy and kindness which I always found in him, telling me, I remember, that he could tell me little himself, but that "the wife" could tell me a great deal, if I saw her. I forget whether he took any steps to acquaint me with "the wife," for I remember that I left Cheyne Row with a flutter of disappointment, feeling that though I had seen the great man, which was no small matter, I was not much the wiser. I remember his tall, thin, stooping figure between the two rooms of the library on the ground floor, in the pleasant shadow of the books, and subdued light and quiet in the place which seemed to supply a very appropriate atmosphere. I did not even know, and certainly never should have learned from any look or tone of his, that I had run the risk of being devoured alive by thus intruding on him. But though I was fluttered by the pride of having seen him, and that people might say "Il vous a parlé, grand'mère," I felt that my hopes were ended and that this was to be all. However, I was mistaken. A day or two after I was told (being still at Mrs Powell's) that a lady whose carriage was at the door begged me to go out and speak to her, Mrs Carlyle. I went, wondering, and found in a homely little brougham a lady with bright eyes and very hollow cheeks, who told me she had to be out in the open air for certain hours every day, and asked me to come and drive with her that we might talk about Irving, whom her husband had told her I wanted to hear about. She must have been over sixty at this time, but she was one of those women whom one never thinks of calling old; her hair was black without a grey hair in it (mine at half the age was already quite grey), her features and her aspect very keen, perhaps a little alarming. When we set off together she began by asking me if I did not come from East Lothian; she had recognised many things in my books which could only come from that district. I had to answer, as I have done on various occasions, that my mother had lived for years in East Lothian, and that I had been so constantly with her that I could never tell whether it was I myself who remembered things or she. This made us friends on the moment; for she too had had a mother, whom, however, she did not regard with all the respect I had for mine. What warmed my heart to her was that she was in many things like my mother; not outwardly, for my mother was a fair radiant woman with a beautiful complexion, and Mrs Carlyle was very dark, with a darkness which was, however, more her meagreness and the wearing of her eager spirit than from nature, or, at least, so I thought,—but in her wonderful talk, the power of narration which I never heard equalled except in my mother, the flashes of keen wit and sarcasm, occasionally even a little sharpness, and always the modifying sense of humour under all.   She told me that day, while we drove round and round the Park, the story of her childhood and of her tutor, the big young Annandale student who set her up on a table and taught her Latin, she six years old and he twenty ("perhaps the prettiest little fairy that ever was born," her old husband said to me, describing this same childhood in his deep broken-hearted voice the first time I saw him after she was gone).   I felt a little as I had felt with my mother's stories, that I myself remembered the little girl seated on the table to be on his level, repeating her Latin verbs to young Edward Irving, and all the wonderful life and hope that were about them,—the childhood and the youth and aspiration never to be measured.   We jogged along with the old horse in the old fly and the steady old coachman going at his habitual jog, and we might have been going on so until now for anything cither of us cared, —she had so much to say and I was so eager to hear.

I have one gift that I know of, and I am a little proud of it.   It is that of making people talk—at least, of making *some* people talk.   My dear Lady Cloncurry says that it is like the art of driving a hoop,—that I give a little touch now and then, and my victim rolls on and on.   But my people who pour forth to me are not my victims, for I love to hear them talk and they take pleasure in it, for the dear talk's sake on both sides, not for anything else; for I have never, I am glad to say, been "a student of human nature" or any such odious thing, nor practised the art of observation, nor spied upon my friends in any way.   My own opinion has always been that I was very unobservant, —whatever I have marked or noted has been done quite unaware; and also, that to study human nature was the greatest impertinence, to be resented whenever encountered.

My friendship with Mrs Carlyle was never broken from this time—it must have been the summer either of 1860 or 1861—till her death. She came to see me frequently, and I spent some (but few) memorable evenings in her house, but at that time did not see her husband again.

January 22.

I have been reading the life of Mr Symonds, and it makes me almost laugh (though little laughing is in my heart) to think of the strange difference between this prosaic little narrative, all about the facts of a life so simple as mine, and his elaborate self-discussions. I suppose that to many people the other will be the more interesting way, just as the movements of the mind are more interesting than those of the body, or rather of the external life. I might well give myself up to introspection at this sad postscript of my life, when all is over for me but the one event to come, which will, I hope and believe, do away with all the suffering past and carry me back, a happy woman, to my family, to a home; though whether it will be like the home on earth who can tell? Nothing can be more sad than the home on earth in which I am now,—the once happy home that rang with my boys' voices and their steps, where everything is full of them, and everything empty, empty, cold, and silent! I don't know whether it is more hard for me to be here with all these associations, or to be in some other place which might not be so overwhelming in its connection with what is past. But it is not a question I need discuss here. Indeed I must not discuss here any question of the kind at all, for any attempt at discussing myself like Mr Symonds, if I were likely to make it, only would end in outlines of trouble, in the deep, deep sorrow that covers me like a mantle. I feel myself like the sufferers in Dante, those of whom we have been reading, who are bent under the weight of stones, though I think I may say with them that *invidiosa non fui;* but this is not to put myself under a microscope and watch what goes on in so paltry a thing, but only the continual appeal I am always making to heaven and earth, consciously or unconsciously, saying often, I know, as I have no right to say, "Is this fair,—is it right that I should be so bowed down to the earth and everything taken from me?" This makes of itself so curious a change even in this quite innocent little narrative of my life. It is so strange to think that when I go it will be touched and arranged by strange hands,—no child of mine to read with tenderness, to hide some things, to cast perhaps an interpretation of love upon others, and to turn over all my papers with the consciousness of a full right to do so, and that theirs is by nature all that was mine. Good Mr Symonds, a pleasant, frank, hearty man, as one saw him from outside! God bless him! for he was kindly to Cecco, who in his tender kindliness made a little pilgrimage to Davos the year after Mr S. died to see his family and offer his sympathy—one of the many unrevealed impulses of kind- ness he had which they never probably guessed at all. But it is vain for me to go on in this strain. I have fallen back into my own way of self-comment, and that is such a different thing.

In the beginning of the winter of 1861 I went to Ealing, and settled down there in a tiny house on the Uxbridge Road. It had a small drawing-room opening on a rather nice garden, a long strip of ground truly suburban, with a pretty plot of grass, a hedge of lilacs and syringas, and vegetables beyond that,—very humble, but I had no pretensions. I think by moments I must have been quite happy here. I remember the cluster of us on the grass, my little Maggie, a little mother in her way, and the two boys. We kept pigeons for the first and only time, and the pretty creatures were fluttering about, and the house standing all open doors and windows, and the sunshine and

F

peace over all. I wrote a few verses, I remember, called "In the Eaves," and had a pang of conscious happiness, always touched with foreboding.

I had gone to Ealing to be near the Blacketts, who, much better off than I and in a much bigger house as became a publisher, lived also in the village, which was not half the size it is now. I had got very intimate with them somehow, I can scarcely tell how. Mrs Blackett was about my age, and a fine creature, very much more clever than her husband, though treated by him in any serious matter as if she had been a little girl,—a thing quite new to me, and which I could not understand. I remember later by some years, at a time when she had got to be very anxious about the education of her boys and he had been somehow moved—a little, perhaps, by myself, impelled in secret by her—to think of sending Arthur to Eton, that while talking it over with me, he suddenly turned to her and said, "Come, Nell, tell me what you think—let us hear your opinion." I remember the frightened look that came on her face, the same look which came over it when she flew before the cow for which she was frightened, and she cried, "Oh, Henry, whatever you think best," and morally ran away, though it was indeed her movement through another which was in reality setting him agoing. Now, why was she afraid of him? He was as good to her as a rather good-humoured but self-important man could be, very fond of her and very proud of her. She was a pretty woman, bright and full of spirit, and much his superior, knowing nothing about books, indeed, but neither did he,—why was she frightened to express an opinion while privately moved very strongly, much more strongly than he was, with the desire to get that important matter decided, and secretly working upon him by all the means at her command? Through their house—planned like so many houses of the same kind, on the system of having everything as expensive as could be got, and making as little show as possible for the money, the latter

not, perhaps, intentional, but from preference for the
humdrum—there fluttered a confused drift from time
to time of literary persons, somewhat small beer like
myself, novel-writers and suchlike. These were all
very literary: our hosts were not literary at all, but
with a business interest in us, along with a certain
kindly contempt, such as publishers generally entertain
for the queer genus writer. It was kindly at least on
the part of the good Blacketts, who were the kindest
folk, he always very brotherly to me, and she most
affectionate. I was very fond of Ellen Blackett, admired her and thought much of her. Their house was
full of big noisy boys, some of them just the same ages as
mine—a great bond between young mothers; handsome
boys, wild and troublesome in later life, but with that
stout commercial thread in them which brings men back
to a life which is profitable when they have sown their
wild oats,—not the highest motive, perhaps, but a re-
cuperative force, such as it was.

I had introduced Mr Blackett by his desire to Miss
Muloch in London,—he, apparently with some business
gift or instinct imperceptible to me, having made out
that there were elements of special success in her.
Probably, however, this instinct was no more than an
appreciation in himself of the sentimentalism in which
she was so strong. He had at once made an arrange-
ment with her, of which 'John Halifax' was the result,
the most popular of all her books, and one which raised
her at once to a high position, I will not say in literature,
but among the novel-writers of one species. She made a
spring thus quite over my head with the helping hand
of my particular friend, leaving me a little rueful,—I
did not at all understand the means nor think very
highly of the work, which is a thing that has happened
several times, I fear, in my experience. Success as
measured by money never came to my share. Miss
Muloch in this way attained more with a few books,
and these of very thin quality, than I with my many.

I don't know why. I don't pretend to think that it
was because of their superior quality. I had, however,
my little success too, while I lived in Ealing. I began
in 'Blackwood' the Carlingford series, beginning with
a story called 'The Doctor's Family,' which I myself
liked, and then 'Salem Chapel.' This last made a
kind of commotion, the utmost I have ever attained
to. John Blackwood wrote to me pointing out how
I had just missed doing something that would have
been made worth the while ; and I believe he was
right, but the chapel atmosphere was new and pleased
people. As a matter of fact I knew nothing about
chapels, but took the sentiment and a few details from
our old church in Liverpool, which was Free Church
of Scotland, and where there were a few grocers and
other such good folk whose ways with the minister
were wonderful to behold. The saving grace of their
Scotchness being withdrawn, they became still more
wonderful as Dissenting deacons, and the truth of the
picture was applauded to all the echoes. I don't know
that I cared for it much myself, though Tozer and the
rest amused me well enough. Then came ' The Perpetual Curate ' and ' Miss Marjoribanks.' I never got
so much praise, and a not unfair share of pudding too.
I was amused lately to hear the comments of Mr David
Stott of Oxford Street, the bookseller, on this. He told
me that he had been in the Blackwoods' establishment
at the time, and of the awe and horror of Mr Simpson
at the prodigal extravagance of John Blackwood in
giving me the price he did, £1500, for ' The Perpetual
Curate.' One could see old Simpson, pale, with the
hair of his wig standing up on his head, remonstrating,
and John Blackwood, magnanimous, head of the house
of Blackwood, and feeling rather like a feudal suzerain,
as he always did, declaring that the labourer was worthy
of his hire. Stott had the air too of thinking it was
sinful extravagance on the editor's part. As for me,
I took what was given me and was very grateful, and

no doubt sang praises to John. On the other side, it was Henry Blackett who turned pale at Miss Muloch's sturdy business-like stand for her money. He used to talk of his encounters with her with affright, very grave, not able to laugh.

This was also the time when I wrote the 'Edward Irving.' It must have been my good time, the little boat going very smoothly and all promising well, and, always my burden of happiness, the children all well. They had the measles, I remember, and were all a little ill the day of the Prince of Wales's marriage, Cyril least ill of all, but feverish one day, when, as I stood over him, putting back his hair from his little hot forehead, he said to me with a pretty mixture of baby metaphor, which I was very proud of and never forgot, "Oh, mamma, your hand is as soft as snow." How like him that was, the poetry and the perception and the tenderness! Cecco too had a momentary illness,— a little convulsion fit which frightened me terribly, one of the few times when I quite lost my head. I remember holding him in his hot bath, and all the while going on calling for hot water and hearing myself do so, and unable to stop it. It was a day on which Mrs Carlyle was coming for the afternoon. When she arrived I was sitting before the fire (though it was summer), with my baby wrapped in a blanket, just out of his bath, and humming softly to him, and he had just startled me out of my misery and made my heart leap for joy, by pulling my face to him with a way he had and saying, all himself again, "Why you singing hum-hum? Sing 'Froggy he would a-wooing go.'" He was only two and a-half. Mrs Carlyle sat by me, so kind and tender and full of encouragement, as if she had known all about babies, but did not stay very long. I think I can see her by the side of the fire, telling me all kinds of comforting things; and by the first post possible that same evening, I got a letter from her telling me that Mr Carlyle had made her sit down at once and write to tell me that a sister of his had once had just such an attack, which never was repeated. God bless them, that much maligned, much misunderstood pair! That was not much like the old ogre his false friends have made him out to be.

Here is a pretty thing. I should like if I could to write what people like about my books, being just then, as I have said, at my high tide, and instead of that all I have to say is a couple of baby stories. I am afraid I can't take the books *au grand sérieux.* Occasionally they pleased me, very often they did not. I always took pleasure in a little bit of fine writing (afterwards called in the family language a "trot"), which, to do myself justice, was only done when I got moved by my subject, and began to feel my heart beat, and perhaps a little water in my eyes, and ever more really satisfied by some little conscious felicity of words than by anything else. I have always had my sing-song, guided by no sort of law, but by my ear, which was in its way fastidious to the cadence and measure that pleased me; but it is bewildering to me in my perfectly artless art, if I may use the word at all, to hear of the elaborate ways of forming and enhancing style, and all the studies for that end.

A good deal went on during that short time at Ealing. I had visitors, Miss Blackwood for two months, and much driving up and down to London to the Exhibition of 1862, which I loathed; but she enjoyed and dragged me, if not at her chariot wheels yet in the "rusty fly," which added very much to my expenses and wasted my time, with the result of being set down by her as very extravagant,—a reproach which has come up against me at various periods of my life. Dr Story came with her, or at least at the same time, and afterwards Principal Tulloch and his wife, whose acquaintance I had made at Edinburgh, St Andrews, and Roseneath in the inter-vening summer of these two years, which I spent at Roseneath, for which I had taken a great fancy—the

beautiful little loch and the hills. I must have gone
then to Willowburn, a small house on a high bank,
with a lovely view of the loch and the opposite shore,
all scattered with houses among the trees, with the
steamboat bustling up and down, and a good deal of
boating and singing and Highland expeditions,—all very
amusing, almost gay, as I had seldom been in my life
before. There was always a youthful party in the manse,
and the Tullochs generally for a time, and various visitors
coming and going,—from the high respectability of Mr
Edward Caird, now Master of Balliol, and Mr Moir, to
all sorts of jocular and light-minded people. I remember
coming home from some wildish expedition, sunburnt
and laden with flowers,—a small group full of fun and
laughter sitting together on deck,—when suddenly the
handsome serious form of Mrs M., always *tirée à quatre
épingles*, always looking propriety itself, was seen slowly
ascending up the cabin stairs, to the confusion and
sudden pallor of myself in particular, to whom she was
coming on a visit. I doubt if I had ever been so gay.
I was still young, and all was well with the children.
My heart had come up with a great bound from all the
strain of previous trouble and hard labour and the valley
of the shadow of death. There was some wit, or at least
a good deal of humour, in the party, and plenty of
excellent talk. The Principal talked very well in those
days—indeed he always did, but never so well as at that
time; and Mr Story, too, was an excellent talker, and his
sister very clever and bright; and my dear *padrona*,[1]
if she never said very much, always quick to see everything, and never able to resist a laugh. We got to have
a crowd of allusions and mutual recollections after all
our boatings and drivings and ludicrous little adventures
on the loch and the hills, which produced a great deal of
laughter even when they were not witty—Jack Tulloch's
appetite, for instance, when he was taken with us on
one occasion, and looked on with exquisite contempt

[1] Mrs Tulloch.

at our admiring raptures over the scenery, but came
to life whenever lunch was going, and was devotedly
attended by the Highland waiters, who entered into the
joke and plied him with dish after dish. He was only
about eleven, poor boy. We were like Farmer Flam-
borough and his daughters, just as much amused by all
these small matters as if they had been the most amusing
things in the world. Miss Blackwood continued to make
part occasionally of our expeditions, and always an
amusing part. She was full of the humour and drollery
of her family, gifts in which they were all strong,
with many little eccentricities of her own, fits of temper
almost always redeemed at the end by a flash of fun
which made the incipient quarrel end in a burst of
laughter.

I worked very hard all the time, I scarcely know how,
for I was always subject to an irruption of merry neighbours bent on some ramble, whom, when they came in
the evening, my big Jane, now more cook than nurse
and general factotum, fed with great dishes of maccaroni,
which she had learned to make in Italy, and which was
our social distinction : everything was extremely primitive at Willowburn. We had one cab in the place,
which took me solemnly now and then to dinner at
the manse and other places, and which was driven by
a certain Andie Chalmers who was our delight, who
spoke in a soft, half-articulate murmur, all vowels,
very tolerant of the pouring rain through which he
drove us occasionally through many a wet mile of road,
allowing with a smile that it was a "wee saft" when
there was a deluge, and who used to come to the cab
door at the foot of a hill with mild insistence, inaccessible
to remonstrance, till we one by one unwillingly, yet
with merry jests, got out to ease the horse.

I suppose after all that I only went for two summers
to Roseneath, but it seems to have bulked very largely
in my life : there was a third later, but that was in
another age, as will be seen, and I was not quite three

years in Ealing. Here I had often with me, as I had a fancy for having, a young lady on a long visit. It would be cruel to name by name the dear good girl, who was brought by her mother to join us one time where we were living, the whole party of us,—myself, big Jane, and the three children. The girl was very tearful and pale, and her mother whispered to me to take no notice, that she had been *praying for strength* to pay me this visit, in which, however, she enjoyed herself very much, I believe. This was, I fear, too good a joke to be kept from my friends.

It was in the summer of 1863 that Geraldine Macpherson came to spend some time with me at Ealing. She was much shattered with Roman fever, and she had a very bad illness of another kind, almost fatal, in my house. The high-spirited creature never gave in, kept her courage and composure through everything, but was as near as possible gone. How one wonders vainly whether, if some one thing like this had not happened, the tenor of one's entire life might have been changed. It was she who persuaded me to go back to Rome when she returned. She persuaded the Tullochs also, to my great surprise, and I daresay their own. The Principal had been ill. It was the first of those mysterious illnesses of his when he fell under the terrible influence of a depression for which there was no apparent cause. He was in the depths of this when he and his wife were with me in 1862, and he told me the whole story of it. It originated (or he thought it did) in (of all things in the world) a false quantity he had made in some Latin passage he had quoted in a speech at some Presbytery or Assembly meeting. He told it with such impassioned seriousness, with his countenance so full of sorrow and trouble, his big blue eyes full of moisture, that I was much impressed, and, I remember, gave him out of my sympathy and emotion the equally inconceivable advice to call the men together to whom that speech had been made, and make a clean breast of it to them. I remem-

ber he was staggered in the extravagance of his talk by
this queer insane suggestion, and perhaps a touch more
would have awakened the man's wholesome humour and
driven the strange delusion away in a shout of laughter;
but I was deadly serious, as was he. He was beginning
to mend, and had been ordered a sea-voyage, and somebody offered him a passage in a Levant steamboat to
Greece. And now, what with Geddie's persuasions and
a spring of eager planning on my part how and when to
go, Mrs Tulloch made up her mind to come to Rome to
meet her husband, then on his way back, bringing her two
eldest girls while he took his eldest boy. There was a
crowd of little children left at home, and I have no doubt
if I heard of such a proceeding now I should think it the
wildest plan. But we carried it out notwithstanding,
with a delightful indifference to ways and means which
makes me shudder when I look back upon it. We set
out the merriest party, ready to enjoy everything, the
padrona, as I soon began to call her, with her daughters
Sara and Fanny, Geddie, myself, my Jane, and the
children, all so small, so happy, so bright, my three little
things—Maggie approaching eleven. We took out a
French governess with us for the sake of the children, a
Mdlle. Coquelin, I think, who soon dropped out of my
life after the great calamity came. But in the meantime
we were all gay, fearing nothing. I remember very distinctly our journey from Paris to Marseilles, because
it was a cheap journey, second class, and monstrous in
length, twenty-seven hours, I think; but we were all very
economical to start with. The endless journey it was!
We were all dead-tired when we arrived, but when we
reached our hotel and got round a table, and well warmed
and refreshed with an innocent champagne, St Peray,
which I made them all drink, our spirits recovered. I
was always great in the way of feeding my party,—would
not hear of teas or coffee meals, but insisted upon meat
and wine, to the horror but comfort of my companions.
That, I believe, was one reason why there were never any

breakdowns among us while travelling. I think with pleasure of the pleasant tumult of that arrival,—the delight of rest, the happy sleepy children all got to bed, the little party of women, all of us about the same age, all with the sense of holiday, a little outburst of freedom, no man interfering, keeping us to rule or formality. I don't know why it should present itself to me under so pleasant a light, for I never liked second-class journeys, nor discomforts of that kind. How often have I travelled that road since, but never so free or light of heart! Heavy and sad are its recollections now, but it is a blessing of God that a happy moment (which is so much rarer) is more conspicuous in life, lighting up the long dreary lane like a lamp, than the sad ones. Oh, the bonnie little dear faces! the rapture of their wellbeing and their happiness, all clinging round mamma with innumerable appeals,—the "bundle of boys," as my Maggie said with sweet scorn, who left no room for her arms to get round me, but only mine round her. I am old and desolate and alone, but I seem to see myself a young mother, the two little fellows in the big fauteuil behind me, clinging round my neck, and their sister at my knee. God bless them, and God bless them,—are they all together now?

We went next day, I think, in the great Messageries steamboat, by Genoa and Leghorn, to Civita Vecchia, and got to Rome in three days, with time enough in Genoa to get a glimpse of the town, and in Pisa next day, making a run from Leghorn. All was well when we got to Rome, where my poor brother William was with Robert Macpherson, helping him to sell his photographs, and pouring out his stores of knowledge upon all the visitors, to good Robert's great admiration. The Tullochs and I got a joint-house in Capo le Case. We had two servants—a delightful *donna da facienda*, called Leonilda, and the only detestable Italian servant I ever saw, Antonio; but the two did everything for us somehow. We had our dinner, I think, from the Trattoria. And we had a month, or a little more, of pleasant life together.   The Principal arrived from Greece—or was it Constantinople ?—and all was well.

Ah me, alas! pain ever, for ever.   This has been the ower-word of my life.   And now it burst into the murmur of pain again.

ROME, 1864.[1]

I did not know when I wrote the last words that I was coming to lay my sweetest hope, my brightest anticipations for the future, with my darling, in her father's grave. Oh this terrible, fatal, miserable Rome!   I came here rich and happy, with my blooming daughter, my dear bright child, whose smiles and brightness everybody noticed, and who was sweet as a little mother to her brothers.   There was not an omen of evil in any way.   Our leaving of home, our journey, our life here, have all been among the brightest passages of my life ; and my Maggie looked the healthiest and happiest of all the children, and ailed nothing and feared nothing,—nor I for her.

Four short days made all the difference, and now here I am with my boys thrown back again out of the light into the darkness, into the valley of the shadow of death. My dearest love never knew nor imagined that she was dying ; no shadow of dread ever came upon her sweet spirit.   She got into heaven without knowing it, and God have pity upon me, who have thus parted with the sweetest companion, on whom unconsciously, more than on any other hope of life, I have been calculating.   I feared from the first moment her illness began, and yet I had a kind of underlying conviction that God would not take my ewe-lamb, my woman-child from me.

The hardest moment in my present sad life is the morning, when I must wake up and begin the dreary world again.   I can sleep during the night, and I sleep as long as I can ; but when it is no longer possible, when

---

[1] These pages, written in Rome at the moment of her bitter grief for the loss of her daughter, seem most suitably inserted here, though Mrs Oliphant left them detached.—ED.

the light can no longer be gainsaid, and life is going on everywhere, then I, too, rise up to bear my burden. How different it used to be! When I was a girl I remember the feeling I had when the fresh morning light came round. Whatever grief there had been the night before, the new day triumphed over it. Things must be better than one thought, must be well, in a world which woke up to that new light, to the sweet dews and sweet air which renewed one's soul. Now I am thankful for the night and the darkness, and shudder to see the light and the day returning.

The Principal calls " In Memorian " an embodiment of the spirit of this age, which he says does not know what to think, yet thinks and wonders and stops itself, and thinks again ; which believes and does not believe, and *perhaps*, I think, carries the human yearning and longing farther than it was ever carried before. Perhaps my own thoughts are much of the same kind. I try to realise heaven to myself, and I cannot do it. The more I think of it, the less I am able to feel that those who have left us can start up at once into a heartless beatitude without caring for our sorrow. Do they sleep until the great day ? Or does time so cease for them that it seems but a matter of hours and minutes till we meet again ? God who is Love cannot give immortality and annihilate affection ; that surely, at least, we must take for granted—as sure as they live they live to love us. Human nature in the flesh cannot be more faithful, more tender, than the purified human soul in heaven. Where, then, are they, those who have gone before us ? Some people say around us, still knowing all that occupies us ; but that is an idea I cannot entertain either. It would not be happiness but pain to be beside those we love yet unable to communicate with them, unable to make ourselves known.

. . . .

The world is changed, and my life is darkened ; and all that I can do is to take desperate hold of this one certainty, that God cannot have done it without reason.

I can get no farther. Sometimes such a longing comes
upon me to go and seek somebody, as I used to go to
Frank to the studio in the old times. But I have nobody
now: my friends are very sorry for me; but there is
nobody in the world who has a right to share my grief,
to whom my grief belongs, as it does to myself—and that
is what one longs for. Sympathy is sweet, but sympathy
is for lighter troubles. When it is a grief that rends one
asunder, one's longing is for the other—the only other
whose heart is rent asunder by the same stroke. For me,
I have all the burden to bear myself. My brother Frank
writes very kindly, speaking as if it were his sorrow too;
but oh, do I not know he will go back among his
unbroken family, and feel all the more glad in his heart
for the contrast of my affliction, and thank God the
more! I don't blame him. I would, perhaps, have
done the same. Here is the end of all. I am alone. I
am a woman. I have nobody to stand between me and
the roughest edge of grief. All the terrible details have
to come to me. I have to bear the loss, the pang
unshared. My boys are too little to feel it, and there is
nobody else in the world to divide it with me. O Lord,
Thou wouldest not have done it but for good reason!
Stand by the forlorn creature who fainteth under Thy
hand, but whom Thou sufferest not to die.

IV.

1894.

ON the 27th of January 1864 my dear little Maggie died of gastric fever. I have written about it all elsewhere. I had escaped, I thought, from the valley of the shadow of death, and had been happy, in sheer force of youth and health and the children: now 'I was plunged again under the salt and bitter waves. I laid her by her father, and it seemed to me that all light and hope were gone from me for ever. Up to five years ago I could not say her dear name without the old pang coming back; since then, when there came to be another to bury in my heart, my little girl seemed all at once to become a tranquil sweet recollection; and now that all are gone she is but a dear shadow, far in the background, while my boys take up in death as in life the whole of the darkened scene. All three gone, and only I left behind! I must try not to dwell on that here. There is enough of distracted thoughts and fancies elsewhere. I have never ventured to go back to Rome. I dared not while I had still the boys to think of. Twice fatal to us, I did not venture to face it a third time. I used to say that if I knew I had a fatal disease, or was sure that they needed me no longer, I would go by myself, and would be happy to die there, but never that they should go. I feel as if I should like to go now, but not to die there, for I must, if it is possible, lie beside my Cyril and Cecco at Eton. But this belongs to a later time.

We left Rome in May, the party still together, the Tullochs and I. I felt that if I left them then I could never bear to see them again; and thus it was that Sara and Fanny Tulloch were left with me for a year, their parents returning home. I remember very little in Rome. The people I met there, the things I saw, seemed all wiped out of my mind, except some strange broken scenes. The first week after that calamity Geddie took me out to Frascati, to their house there, for a little change; and I never can forget the aspect of that summer place, where we had once lived through the hot July and August, in the desolation of the winter and of my misery. We were on the upper storey of a great cold Italian house, the cold penetrating to the heart, cold such as never was seen or felt surely in the North,—no servants, no comforts, sitting crying over the fire through a dismal day or two in a great, gaunt, half-empty room, my heart breaking for the children. It did not last long, but I have never forgotten these dismal days. There is another day in my memory like a dream. It was then March, and we had gone to Albano and were living there. The Macphersons came out to visit us, and, as they could never be without company, asked some of their friends out from Rome on the Sunday to go to Nemi. Then, finding how I shrank from the strangers, Robert took me through the woods,—a wonderful, wild, beautiful way,—leading my donkey to the place where we were to dine. I recollect a kind of soothing in the sensation of the spring, the wild freshness of the wood; a party of charcoal-burners, whose encampment we passed, appear to me like a picture,—wild men, not safe to meet, but my kind old Robert knew them all and their dialect and their ways. Nemi, the wonderful blue lake, bound within the circle of its deep banks, and an old Palazzo with frescoed rooms looking sheer down into the wonderful metallic water, which looked something like molten sapphires, but of a warmer colour. I had half a mind, I remember, to take an *appartamento* in that house, and throw myself into the rut of artist life, though my instincts were not of that kind,—a life not exactly disorderly, but a little wild and wandering and gregarious. I wonder, if I had stayed at Nemi, and brought the boys up so—how bewildering the thought is of things one might have done.

After that we went to Naples and Capri, where we stayed a long time and got to know all the guides and people, riding about every day over all the lower island and up to Anacapri—all like a dream. And Sentella, the good hunchback maid whose face the Principal said was so full of moral beauty, and Feliciello, who was not by any means so good, but whom we liked and petted. I wrote, I think, a little sketch of it afterwards, called "Life on an Island," or some such name, in 'Blackwood.'[1]

In May we left Rome finally and moved northward to the Lake of Como, where we stayed at Bellaggio; then into Switzerland, where we spent the summer, chiefly on the Lake of Geneva; then to Paris, where we passed the winter. The Principal and the *padrona* had gone home long before, and my party in Paris consisted of my two little boys, the two girls, Sara and Fanny, Jane, and a Swiss - French governess, Mademoiselle Pricam, whom we had picked up at Montreux. In Paris we got a cheerful apartment on the Champs Elysées, the sunny side. It was at the height of the gaiety and prosperity of the Empire, and I used to say that the sight of all the gay stream of life from the windows, all the fine people coming and going, the brightness and the movement, were a kind of salvation to me in that dark and clouded time. I remember going off to St Germain to spend the first anniversary of my Maggie's death, taking my delightful boy with me; and the dark gloomy evening after I had put him to bed in the inn, once more sitting desolate and

---

[1] "Life on an Island," 'Maga,' January 1865.

crying over the fire; but next morning the terrace
in the wintry sunshine, and all the thoughts that came
to one then, and still more the going back to the
cheerful rooms in Paris, which were a kind of home,
and my other dear little fellow rushing with his shout
of welcome to mamma, brought a little sunshine back;
though it was not till the 4th of April after that, when
I found the rooms crowded with flowers which they
had all gone out to get for me on my birthday before
I was up, that I began to feel as if I had passed again
from death into life. I took them all out to St Cloud
in reward for their flowers, and they were all so gay,
and the morning and the drive so bright.

In Paris I saw a good deal of the Montalemberts.
I have described how I translated the Count's book when
I first went to Scotland after my widowhood. He had
been pleased with it, I don't know why, for it was badly
done; and by John Blackwood's desire and introduction
came to see me in Paris, and I dined there once or
twice, though under protest, for I had never gone anywhere or cared to see anybody. There was one party
I remember which was interesting, where were Prévost-
Paradol and some other literary people. I was too
shy and out of my element to make much of them,
and have never been proud of my French; so I did
not get the good I ought out of this glimpse of society.
On one occasion Miss Blackwood, who came to Paris
and paid me a long visit, was with me,—a little alarming in her large bare shoulders in the small party with
the other ladies all decorously covered. There was, I
remember, a pretty graceful Madame L'Abbadie, whose
husband came up to me, a man with a dreadful brogue,
and said, " I speak English better than Montalembert;
the reason is I am born in Dublin, and he is born in
London." Montalembert's English was delightful, perfect in accent and idiom; I don't remember any mistake
of his except the amusing and flattering one with which
he expressed his surprise when we first met to find me

"not so respectable" as he had supposed. I daresay
it was a mistake made on purpose; for to be sure I
was still young, and perhaps, in the still lingering exaltation of my sorrow and the tears that were never far off
from my eyes, looked younger than I was. It was then
1865, and I must have been thirty-seven, and had grey
hair. Montalembert himself was, I think, one of the
most interesting men I ever met. He had that curious
mixture of the—shall I say?—supernaturalist and man
of the world (not mystic, he was no mystic, but yet
miraculous, if there is any meaning in that) which has
always had so great an attraction for me, — keen and
sharp as a sword, and yet open to every belief and to
every superstition, far more than I ever could have
been, who looked at him and up to him with a sort
of admiring wonder and yet sympathy, not without a
smile in it. He was a little like Laurence Oliphant
in this, but Laurence was not a highly educated man
like Montalembert. M. de Montalembert struck me as
the most delightful, benign, and genial of men when
I saw him first; but afterwards I used to say that
he was one of the few men I was afraid of, and that
he had a fine way of picking one up as on some polished pair of tongs, and holding one up to the admiration of the world around, in all the bloom of one's
foolishness. I remember on one occasion, when there
was great talk of vacant fauteuils in the Académie, and
of the candidates, two of whom in particular were being
discussed, I asked him, rather sillily, whether there were
two vacancies or two candidates for one vacancy—something of that sort,—when he turned to the company and
called their attention to the orderly, temperate, English
mind, in which there was no rush at a prize, but a well-
balanced competition of two, as I had suggested. There
was a great deal of laughter, in which, of course, any
shy explanation of mine was completely drowned. I
doubt whether an Englishman of equally fine manners
would have held up a French stranger to the gentle

ridicule of the company in this way. And yet I always liked him in the midst of my alarm, and he was very kind. I gave him the 'Life of Irving,' with a little protest, which was quite true, that it was not because I had written it, but because of the man Irving that I wished him to read it, which protest he received with a little banter and look of seeing through me; but afterwards avowed that he was touched by the character of Irving and its truth, mightily apart as it was from all his own prepossessions, which were so strong, however, that he could not bear Scotland,—could not even persuade himself to permit the glamour of Sir Walter to excuse the black anti-Catholic desolation of that dreadful country, all but Iona. Happening to speak of Carlyle, he expressed great dislike for him. I had mentioned that unfortunately Carlyle had no children. "Why unfortunately?" said Montalembert; "happily, rather, for he was not a man to have the bringing up of children." I made some sort of indignant reply, but added, "I don't believe in education." He paused a moment, laughed, and said, "Neither do I." Carlyle had an equal dislike of him, and shot forth a thunderbolt at him on one occasion when I mentioned him; but spoke of Lamennais in a half tender tone,—" There is no hairm in him, no hairm in him," he said. Lamennais was tragic from the Montalembert point of view, —a name to be spoken of with bated breath.

It was Count de Montalembert who gave me tickets for one of the side chapels in Notre Dame, where Père Félix was preaching to men during Lent,—a scene I have described somewhere, and which I read a description of lately in the life of Mrs Craven. The nave was packed closely with men, a dark mass, their immovable faces whitening the whole surface of that great area under the not abundant lights, and the spare figure of the monk in the pulpit, his face whiter still, like ivory. It was very dark in the side chapels, and we did not hear very well; but the sight was very impressive, and specially

so on, I think, the Thursday of Holy Week, when this
immense crowd of men sang the Stabat Mater in unison,
—the most wonderful volume of sound, which was quite
overwhelming in the depth and strength of it, rolling
like a kind of regulated and tempered thunder, or like
the sound of many waters,—a perfectly new and extraordinary effect. (I remember finding out afterwards,
to my great confusion, that these tickets had been given
to me only for one night, and that I had kept other
people out of them—the sort of horrible ridiculous want
of sense which makes one hot all over when one dis-
covers it.)

On the Easter morning we went very early to Notre
Dame to see the communion of these men, which was
also a very touching sight. There was an old lady in
the gallery where we were who looked down all the time,
crying and talking to herself, "Dix soldats—et un petit
bon homme en blouse." I, more profane, smiled a little,
and was a little ashamed of myself for doing so, at the
air of conscious solemnity with which most of the men
came up to the altar, very devout, but yet with a certain sense of forming part of a very great and ennobling
spectacle.

I made little of the ladies of the Montalembert household on this occasion, my attention being chiefly attracted
to him. The girls were quite young, and I did not see
enough of them to make friends as afterwards with
Madame de Montalembert,—a person to whom it is difficult to do justice in words, the fine, ample, noble Fla-
mande, *grande dame au bout des ongles*, ready and capable
to do anything in the world of which there might be
need, to defend a castle, or light a fire, or nurse the
sick, but helplessly unable to "do" her own hair,—a
characteristic failure which amused me much when I
found it out, which was not, however, till much later.
As usual I did not make half the use of my opportunities
which I ought to have done, was shy of going to see
them, and held back generally after my fashion, which

I always regret afterwards. I am not sure that I ever saw Montalembert again.

At the other end of the social scale we picked up a curious pair in Paris,—a man who was an Oxford man, far from a refined specimen, indeed, who advertised in 'Galignani' for pupils, and whom I engaged to begin my boy with Latin. He came, I think, every morning, and Cyril, aged eight, began his serious education under him. He was of a species of which I saw various specimens later,—the half rustic, half vulgar son of a country clergyman, gone all wrong at the University, but not a bad scholar, and, above all, not a bad man—coarse, red-faced, perhaps a little vicious, certainly addicted to drink. He had a wife, a kind of falsely pretty creature, or with a false air of being pretty, very pink and white, with one leg a little shorter than the other in consequence of some illness, who had come to Paris to be under Nèlotan, the great doctor. There was a baby and an English, or rather Welsh, nurse, who stood by them through thick and thin, strongly disapproving of both, but faithful all the same. It was she, I think, probably through Jane, from whom we heard how the man —— had been engaged to his wife before her illness, and had helped to nurse her through it and made light of the defect it left, which he would not permit to interfere with their marriage. This prepossessed me much in his favour. Then came the report that she had a dreadful temper, and threw plates and cups at him in her fury, which made his good-humour and apparent devotion to her more touching still. Afterwards it appeared that she had a tolerable income and he not a penny, besides being in innumerable scrapes, which discouraged us a little. They used to come and spend one evening in the week with us, and I think —— did his preliminary teaching very well. Fanny was his pupil too, as well as Cyril; they were both, it is true, exceptional scholars.

We had another regular evening visitor once a-week—

a man whom, though I never saw more of him than those regular weekly visits, I got to think of as a dear friend, and I think he had the same sort of feeling for me— Giovanni (or, as he wrote himself, John) Ruffini, the author of 'Dr Antonio,' an Italian refugee of the 1848 times, and for years a resident in London, where he had written that delightful book in English. His written English was beautiful, but he spoke it badly and with difficulty. He was a large mild man, with blue eyes, heavy-lidded and large — large externally, and specially remarkable when they were cast down, which sounds odd but was true. He lived with an English family, with whom he had been for years—partly brother, partly lover, partly guest. I did not know them, and I don't know the rights of the story. The father had died some time before, but he still kept his place among them, and went about with the mother of the house, both of them growing old with what seemed to me a delightful innocence and naturalness. They made their *villeggiatura,* these two together, sometimes in a couple of chalets on a Swiss mountain, as if there had not been such a thing as an evil tongue in the world, which interested me exceedingly; and indeed his weekly visit, his pensive Italian mildness, the look of the traditional exile, though in so perfectly natural a man, was very interesting: that exile look with the faint air of fiction in it, and its absolute sincerity all the same, has gone out of mortal ken nowadays.

Another queer pair that I used to see were old Father Prout (Mahony, or O'Mahony, as he called himself) and the old lady about whom he circled, and who was a very quaint old lady indeed, with the air of having been somebody,—a very dauntless, plain-spoken old person in old shiny black satin and lace, and looking as if everything was put on as well as the satin—hair, teeth, and everything else. I don't know if there had been anything wrong in the connection—it was certainly patriarchal then,—they were so old and such *bons camarades,*

and so entirely at ease with each other. It was wicked
of me, I fear, but it amused me to think that these old
people had perhaps indulged in a *grande passion* and
defied the world for each other. I thought no worse of
them, somehow, which I am aware is a most immoral
sentiment. But perhaps there had never been anything
in the least wrong. Peace to their ancient ashes!—they
were a strange pair. She—I have forgotten her name
—came to see me, and I went to her house once in the
evening, somewhere in the heart of Paris, up a great
many stairs, where she had an apartment exactly like
herself, with much dingy decoration and a great many
curious things, and the air somehow of being dressed
like its mistress, and scented and done up with an arti-
ficialness which, as in the lady's case, by dint of long
continuance had grown to be perfectly sincere. She
bade her old gentleman sing me his great song, "The
Bells of Shandon," which he did, standing up against
the mantelpiece, with his pale head, like carved ivory,
relieved against the regular *garniture de cheminée*, the
big clock and candelabra. He had a fine face with
delicate features, almost an ascetic face, though his life
had been not exactly of that description, I fear. He
was an unfrocked priest, and I think was one of the
Fraser group, which was, more or less, an imitation
of the Blackwood group, with much real or pretended
rivalry, and had knocked about a great deal in his life,
and was poor. I think I heard that the old lady died,
and that he became poorer still. There were thus two
elderly romances, in old fidelity and friendship, under
my eyes, made innocent, almost infantile, especially in
the latter case, as of old babies, independent of sex and
superior to it, amid all the obliterations of old age. I
had several curious visitors of this kind, chiefly sent to
me, I think, by Robert Macpherson,—one of them Miss
Cushman, the actress, whom I had met in London and
had not liked, but who touched my heart with her
evident deep knowledge of trouble and sorrow. I think

I have described her and others in some other places, though I can't tell where. I had visitors too from home,—Mrs Fitzgerald, Miss Blackwood, and Principal Tulloch, who came to take the girls home, and in his turn brought some odd Scotch - cosmopolitan people. Not cosmopolitan, however, was the Scotch minister, who held his little conventicle in the Oratoire, and who said sturdily, and with the courage of his opinion, that he had not learned French, and did not mean to do so, as he disapproved of it altogether.

We were about six months in Paris, in the little bright apartment which I remember cost over a thousand francs for wood and coal during that time, and was as warm as a nest. The party consisted of the two girls, my two dear little boys,—Cyril so full of wit and fun, Cecco always so original even in his babyhood, learning to read in Mademoiselle's wonderful way in a fortnight without a tear,—Mademoiselle herself, Jane, and a servant and a half—the *bonne à tout faire* and her child. The Champs Elysées, full of sun and brightness and fine carriages, and all the fine people passing in a stream every after-noon, did me much good, and it all bears a radiant aspect now as I look back, heavy though my heart often was. I heard then for the first time of our after-wards familiar and beloved cousin Annie, in reality a second cousin, whom I had never seen, but who wrote introducing herself to me, with some literary aspirations, taking at that time the shape of poetry, against which I remember I advised her, suggesting a novel instead. I cannot remember what I was then doing, nor how I was in the matter of money, but I presume I must have been going on with a flowing sail, working a great deal and not requiring to take much thought of my expenses, which, alas! was my way. I ought to have been saving, of course, but I didn't, with a miraculous ease of mind which some people have thought criminal. I sometimes think, too, that it was so, and also have sometimes lately (1895) pondered upon a sadder[1] theory still, as if that had something to do with the great sorrows that have clouded the end of my life. I never had any expensive tastes, but loved the easy swing of life, without taking much thought for the morrow, with a faith in my own power to go on working, which up to this time has been wonderfully justified, but which has been a great temptation and danger to me all through in the way of economies. I had always a conviction that I could make up by a little exertion for any extra expense. Sickness, incapacity, want of health or ability to work, never occurred to me, I suppose. At the same time, I never was very highly paid for my work, and perhaps this had its effect too on my carelessness in pecuniary matters. I made enough to carry me on easily, almost luxuriously, but not enough to save, never a large sum which could be partly put away at once and give one a taste of the sweetness of possessing something. I could not do this, and I fear it was not in me to practise that honourable pinching and sparing by which some women do so much. I had not the time for it, nor, indeed, I am ashamed to say, the wish. I am ashamed too to make the confession that I do not in the

---

[1] This is what I thought—that I had so accustomed them to the easy going on of all things, never letting them see my anxieties or know that there was a difficulty about anything, that their minds were formed to that habit, that it took all thought of necessity out of my Cyril's mind, who had always, I am sure, the feeling that a little exertion (always so easy *to-morrow*) would at any time set everything right, and that nothing was likely ever to go far wrong so long as I was there. The sentiment was not ungenerous, it was in a way forced upon him, partly by my own *insouciance* and partly by the fact that he was always saved from any practical effect of foolishness, so that at the last, what with the growth of habit, there was no other way for it but that,— "There is no way but this," words I used to say over to myself. And my Cecco, who had not these follies, but who was stricken by the hand of God, until that too rendered further going on impossible, by the drying up of my sources and means of getting anything for him—so that I seem sometimes to feel as if it were all my doing, and that I had brought by my heedlessness both to an *impasse* from which there was no issue but one. It was a kind of forlorn pleasure to me that they had never wanted anything, but this turns it into a remorse. Who can tell? God alone over all knows, and works by our follies as well as our better ways. Must it not be at last to the good of all?

least remember what I was working at at this time. It is not that I have ever been indifferent to my work. I have always been most grateful to God that it was work I liked and that interested me in the doing of it, and it has often carried me away from myself and quenched, or at least calmed, the troubles of life. But perhaps my life has been too full of personal interests to leave me at leisure to talk of the creatures of my imagination, as some people do, or to make believe that they were more to me in writing than they might have been in reading—that is, my own stories in the making of them were very much what other people's stories (but these the best) were in the reading. I am no more interested in my own characters than I am in Jeanie Deans, and do not remember them half so well, nor do they come back to me with the same steady interest and friendship. Perhaps people will say this is why they never laid any special hold upon the minds of others, though they might be agreeable reading enough. But this does not mean that I was indifferent to the work as work, or did not beat it out with interest and pleasure. It pleases me at this present moment, I may confess, that I seem to have found unawares an image that quite expresses what I mean — *i.e.*, that I wrote as I read, with much the same sort of feeling. It seems to me that this is rather an original way of putting it (to disclose the privatest thought in my mind), and this gives me an absurd little sense of pleasure.

We left Paris in the summer — my little boys, the governess, Jane, and I. I did not want to go back to England till the end of the year, and we strayed about a little. The tutor aforesaid and his wife had taken a house in Normandy with the intention of having boarders, and there it occurred to me to go for a short time — especially while Jane went home for her holiday. The house called itself the Château de Montilly, which sounded well. It was, however, a new square house in a garden, without any attractions what-

ever; and the unfortunate pair were rather insufferable
at such close quarters, and I was very thankful to get
away in about a fortnight — staying that time merely
for decency's sake. Mr Story, who was in Paris, came
down to visit me, I remember; and we went to see
Bayeux and the tapestry, jogging along in a country
shandrydan with a huge red umbrella. That fact and
a wonderful thunderstorm there was — which he and I
sat at an open window to watch, much to the annoyance and terror of our hosts, who would have liked to
shut it out with bolted shutters—are about all I recollect, except the discomfort of the forced stay with
people totally out of my way and kind, and the little
meannesses of the household, and the annoyed interest
we began to take in what there would be for dinner
as soon as we discovered that the fare was sure to be
scanty and bad. We escaped as soon as we could,
having taken in a few views of French village life,
and made the discovery that to take out an ill-tempered
Mrs —— for a little diversion—even if it were no more
exciting than a Norman fair, and the drive thereto in
a carriole—was good for her soul's health, poor thing,
and cleared the skies. I am a little hazy about what
followed. We went to Avranches, to the little country
town hotel, where the good people of the place came
in to dine, and tied their dinner napkins round their
half-finished bottles of wine; and we went to Mont St
Michel, which delighted me, and where I had half a
mind to take one of the many empty houses left by
the prison officials when it ceased to be a prison. One
imposing white house dominating the village I was told
I could have for a hundred francs a-year! There would
have been economy, and a certain amount of interest
and picturesque surroundings, but the sea and the vast
sands were very grey. We bivouacked in an almost
empty house, containing little but what are called box-
beds in Scotland, and a table and chair or two, which
belonged to an old priest, very snuffy and shabby, who

was called M. L'Aumonier, and had, I suppose, filled
that office in the economy of the great prison, though
I don't quite know what office it is. He took me to
window after window to show me little shelves of garden
which he had on the slopes of the rock—one here and
another there, but each provided with certain conveni-
ences, on which the good man insisted much. The
first night there I was seized by a sudden panic to find
that I had lodged myself and my helpless little party
in the midst of a strange, unknown, and rather rough
community—in a house which had not a key even to
its outer door,—and sat up till daylight to watch over
them. The light reassured me, and the thought of my
big and dauntless Jane, who was worth two men, and
who would have faced an army for her two little boys.
Oh, my little boys! and the happiness of watching
over them and all their ways and sayings, though I
was sad enough then, thinking there was no sadder
mother, longing for my Maggie wherever I went.

We spent a long time at St Adresse, near Havre, in
a house which belonged to Queen Christina of Spain,
where there was capital sea-bathing; and the children,
or at least Cyril, began to learn to swim, and enjoyed
themselves in all the amusements of the sea-side. One
half tragic experience we had. Setting out to row, I
and my little man, only eight, with a recklessness which
I shiver now to think of, we were caught by the current,
and had not our plight been seen from the shore and
a man sent after us, I don't know what might have
happened. The current was well known, only not to
me, newly arrived and, as it appeared, very imprudent.
We had rowed a great deal on the Gairloch, and we
were close inshore, and the shining sunlit water looked
like burnished glass or gold, or both. Mademoiselle
was with us, and as bold as a little stout Swiss lion.
I had luck in that way at least. How much would have
been spared if that boat had drifted out to sea! many
years' toil coming to so little, many years' misery and

sorrow, though many happy too—and this long tragedy
at the end! To have ended all together under that
rippled sheet of gold, what an escape from all that came
after! But it would have been hard on Mademoiselle
and her old mother at Lausanne. It makes one's head
go round, however, to think how little difference it would
have made had such a little catastrophe taken place,
and made a paragraph in the papers,—an innocent, not
undesirable, not unlovely catastrophe, all over sweetly
and suddenly that has taken so many years to get over,
and yet is over or soon will be : how little important to
any one else ! probably so much better for ourselves !
I feel a kind of envy now of the situation and of the
possibility—but this is all so vain.

I suppose it must have been after St Adresse that
we went to St Malo, where the delightful bay, crowded
with rocky islets and downy white sails, delighted me.
We found a small cabin of a house on the very edge of
the cliff at Dinard, which was then a little village, very
primitive and quiet, whence we crossed to St Malo in a
small boat with a big sail,—always somewhat alarming
to me, notwithstanding my rash boating. It was called
the *bateau de poissage*, I remember, in the Norman-French
that always sounded to me like Scotch. We had a noble
Marie for our *bonne*, a woman with the finest thoughtful
face, whom I had photographed in her beautiful cap, in
spite of her protestations that it would have been much
better to take her niece, a commonplace, pretty little
girl. Probably they do not wear those caps now, in
which they looked like medieval princesses, wandering
after the procession of the *Fête Dieu*, which took place
while we were there. But these are all very trivial
recollections. I remember being extremely touched by
the playing of the local band in the Dinard church,
I suppose on this occasion. They played where the
anthem would come in in the English service, and what
they played was *Ah che la morte*, and other airs from
the "Trovatore," which shocked me at first into the

usual English sense of superiority, and then affected me
greatly with the thought that it was absolutely the best
thing they could do which they were offering to God,
whether very worthy or not, and what could the finest
genius do more? My other best recollection is of the
country doctor, whom I called to see my dear little
Cecco in some illness, just enough to make an anxious
woman more anxious, and who laughed and prescribed
the *galette* of the place, a kind of cracknel, and *confiture*
and cider, the drink of the place. I could have hugged
him for his laugh, which proved how little was the
matter, and administered the cracknel and the jam, but
not the cider, which was sour. So little a thing dwells
on one's mind, but it was not little at that moment,
when these infantile vicissitudes were the most important matters in life.

We had rather a wild, rather a wearisome, but in some
ways an amusing, journey from St Malo to Boulogne.
There was a boat direct from St Malo, which, if I had
been a wise woman, I should have taken, and so got
home quite cheaply. But I had a great dislike to the
sea; and with some compunction for the expense and
more pleasure in the adventure,—though adventure there
was really none, except that the manner of the journey
was by that time a little out of the way,—we set off by
land. So far as I remember, we went sixty miles the
first day, if that is possible, but I don't recollect where
we halted or how many days we took to the journey
altogether. We started with that perfect ignorance of
where we were going, and perfect confidence that everything would go well, which, I suppose, is peculiar to
women (when they are not nervous and timorous). The
carriage was packed with toys and books and all kinds
of things for the children, and the progress through the
air, the little exhilaration of the start, the glimpse of
village interiors as we rattled past, the arrivals and
departures, were quite enough amusement for me. I
suppose Mademoiselle must have liked it too, for she

threw herself completely into the frolic. And as for
Jane, it was all in the day's work to her. I think we
passed one night at Granville. I remember distinctly
that we all lunched in the middle of the day at an
unknown and nameless village, upon potatoes *en robe
de chambre*, which Mademoiselle sagely advised as a
thing we could be quite sure of, whereas other dishes
might be doubtful, and the fragrant tray of fresh sponge
biscuits, taken warm and sweet out of the oven while we
were there and added to our meal as desert, which made
me feel that the capabilities of the place were greater
than we thought. The rush across a broad level of
country without many features was monotonous in the
end; but the quiet and fresh air, and long silences and
sense of progress, were all soothing and pleasant. I have
a kind of shadowy recollection of the journey, like a
dream, that is refreshing still. We spent a day or two in
Dieppe, intending at first to take the boat there, but having
got into the habit of driving, with the old delightful connections of the *vetturino* coming back, we finally decided
to continue our drive along the coast to Boulogne, and,
though we did not deserve it, were rewarded at last by
the smoothest of passages across the Channel—a thing
which in those days I always dreaded. We found rooms
in London in the Bayswater Road, opposite Kensington
Gardens—a place I have always liked; and then I set to
work to find a home for us, where there should be means
of education for the boys. My mind was at first inclined for Harrow, but something, I forget what, induced
me to come to Windsor, which captivated me at once.
Either then or later I wrote a letter to Mr Warre, now
the Head Master, then young and "rising," whom I
found very agreeable, and who decided, but with some
reluctance, that it might be possible to educate my sons
at Eton in all respects like the other boys there, but sleeping at home; which possibility, combined with the beauty
of the river and the castle, and the air of cheerful life
about, decided me very quickly to settle here. And a

house was found very quickly; not this in which I now sit, and where almost all the events of my later life have taken place, but one in the same Crescent, within two doors of me, smaller than this. We came into it in November, I think, 1865. I have been here ever since. The house was very bright, the sun on it almost from its rising to its setting, a pleasant little garden behind, and the Crescent garden—a piece of ground of considerable extent, which we called, I don't know why, the plantation, beautifully planted, and, considering its position, a wonderful little piece of landscape gardening,—of which we took possession by acclamation. Very few people used it in these days : the day of lawn-tennis was not yet, and I suppose most of the people were elderly, for we had it almost altogether to ourselves. I never knew till a long time after of how much importance it was in the first chapter of my boys' life, this bit of town garden with its fine trees and wild nooks and corners. Lately my Cecco has told me of so many things that were done there, "when we were small," as he always said. It lies under my windows now, but I can't trust myself to go into it.

Here we got to know gradually various people about. The Hawtreys, a family of old brothers and sisters, relatives of the old Provost Hawtrey of Eton, were in themselves a very characteristic household. They lived in a large red-brick house near the church, the centre of an enormous connection, married brothers and sisters, nephews and nieces innumerable. The Windsor portion of the family were known universally by their Christian names, Stephen and Anna, Henry and Florence. They have all lived in my ken to be very old people,—the two first having both died over eighty, while the younger pair still survive, still ascending towards the snows. It was a house full of entertainment, of family gatherings, Christmas festivities, in which the overwhelming atmosphere of Hawtreyism pervaded everything. They were all kind naturally, but anything so bland as John Hawtrey,

H

who was an Eton master, or so effusively benignant as old Stephen, I never saw. The last was full of schemes, almost always benevolent, always more or less as people thought, profitable, as exemplified in certain transactions which are not worth telling, which were mere gossip, though if I had time or was sure to give pain to nobody, they were not without amusing points. A wicked wag at Eton declared that Stephen got up in the morning to build the walls of his new mathematical school out of the materials which were lying ready for more slothful workmen to build Mr Somebody's house hard by,—a story everybody laughed at as *ben trovato*, though I cannot say I ever knew these good people to do anything to the disadvantage of their neighbours. They were good people, whether or no. They had all kinds of parties continually going on,—dinner-parties, garden-parties, musical-parties. In one of the last a family quartette played what was rather new and terrible to me, long sonatas and concerted pieces, which filled my soul with dismay. It is a dreadful confession to make, and proceeds from want of education and instruction, but I fear any appreciation of music I have is purely literary. I love a song and a " tune "; the humblest fiddler has sometimes given me the greatest pleasure, and sometimes gone to my heart ; but music properly so called, the only music that many of my friends would listen to, is to me a wonder and a mystery. My mind wanders through andantes and adagios, gaping, longing to understand. Will no one tell me what it means ? I want to find the old unhappy far - off things or battles long ago, which Wordsworth imagined in the Gaelic song. I feel out of it, uneasy, thinking all the time what a poor creature I must be. I remember the mother of the sonata players approaching me with beaming countenance on the occasion of one of those performances, expecting the compliment which I faltered forth, doing my best not to look insincere. " And I have that every evening of my life ! " cried the triumphant woman. " Good heavens ! and you have

survived it all this time," was my internal comment. I
can see the kind glow on her face and the mother's pride,
and thought myself, I am glad to say, a very poor
creature to be left so helplessly behind, though not without a rueful amusement too.

I had a little neighbour in one of the smaller Crescent
houses, whom the children soon got to call Aunt Nelly,
and I "Little Nelly,"—I hardly know why, unless for
the too perfect reason that she was Nelly and very little,
which of course was much too simple to be the true
meaning of the name. She it was who, dying in her
sleep without so much as the movement of a finger—
little happy woman, always of the angel kind—put the
story, if story it can be called, of "The Little Pilgrim"
into my mind. Many simple people here had a sort of
grotesque notion that there was something of her in it
more than the suggestion, as if, alas! it were possible to
follow and describe the ways of those who are gone.
She was far from being wise or clever, generally reputed
rather a silly little woman; but with a heart of gold,
and a straightforward, simple, right judgment, which
was always to me like the clear shining of a tiny light.
She *was*, perhaps, a silly little woman, in fact, in some
ways. There are kinds of foolishness I like for my own
part, as there is also a kind of benignant gentle dulness
which always soothes me, and which I constantly recom-
mend as so good a relief from the intellectualism some of
my friends love; but then they do love the intellectual,
and I don't—much. My little Nelly had been trained
to be unselfish, which, being far better than unselfish
without training, was the only little fictitious trait in her
—but so superficial and innocent. I often point the
moral to the girls of that kind of technical unselfishness,
by telling how little Nelly on a muddy road exhausted
herself in finding a dry part for me, while she hobbled
through the mud, as if I was to be outdone in that cheap
generosity! But the woman was of the angel kind, and
breathed goodness round her. She was the guardian,

when I first knew her, of an old, old mother, whose
head and memory were gone, and of a brother with a
nervous disease — a poor man cast out of life in the
middle of his days, and feeling himself to the bottom
of his heart a cumberer of the soil.   Her life was spent
in amusing and caring for these two invalids, playing
cards for hours with them.   My little Cecco used to
go in the evening, rather proud of being wanted, seven
or eight years old, in his little velvet suit, to make the
fourth at whist, and when he was a man would speak
of the long whist "which was Aunt Nelly's way."   The
invalid brother was rarely visible, but sometimes I found
a bouquet of flowers laid on my balcony, which was low
enough to be reached from outside, which he laid there,
stealing unnoticed into the garden.

Both these poor people died after long years, and left
my little Nelly free — to take other burdens on her
shoulders, and save other wounded creatures of God.
Once when I was in great straits, and very anxious
and unhappy, I asked her to help me in praying for
the great boon I desired.   I am not of the kind who
do that usually, and perhaps when the trouble had been
softened away I forgot even that I had done it; but
thinking of it all years after, in the great and deep joy
of knowing that the change I desired had come to pass,
though without knowing what had led to it, I suddenly
remembered how in my trouble I had sought her help,
and it seemed to me like a flash of light upon the road
by which we had come, not knowing.   I have never
asked any one else to do that for me.

Notwithstanding, she was the object of perpetual
banter in the house.   There was almost always some
current joke about what little Nelly had done or said,
at which she herself was the first to laugh.   How many
of those foolish, dear, affectionate mockeries I remember!
Not mockeries—the word is too harsh: the ring of the
laughter, the shining of the young eyes, and the light in
her own, as beautiful as the youngest eyes among them,

worn and faded as she was, are as fresh as ever. I wonder
sometimes if what has been ever dies! Should not I find
them all round the old whist-table, and my Cecco, with
his bright face and the great blue vein that showed on
his temple, proud to be helping to amuse the old people,
if I were but bold enough to push into the deserted house
and look for them now? I have so often felt, with a
bewildered dizziness, as if that might be.

Then there was another near neighbour, one whom I
have seen to-day, who lives on as I do, lonely and forlorn, with all the elements in her then of a brilliant life,
—clever, witty, pretty, a woman not to be passed over,
and who, had her lot fallen otherwise, might have filled
any position almost, and perhaps been a leader of
society, had life been more auspicious to her. When
I knew her first she lived in one of the most important houses in the place, with a delightful old mother,
in a delightful house and much apparent comfort. She
had a handsome son in London, a beautiful daughter
who had made a distinguished marriage abroad. She
herself had read a great deal, was an accomplished
musician, spoke the purest French, knew foreign society
tolerably well, and had been one of the "county"
people more or less, but when I knew her first was
very lonely, not in perfect intelligence either with son
or daughter, and either negligent or frettingly, insuffer-
ably kind and anxious over her mother. I don't know,
and have never desired to know, notwithstanding the
eagerness of many people to inform me, what her past
had been. It was not the least a past such as is now
meant when a woman with a past is spoken of, but
there had been some foolish rash attempt to secure
a very brilliant marriage at home for the beautiful
daughter, which had prejudiced the little society about
against her, and she was very solitary, her mother old
and an invalid, one of the prettiest and most charming
old ladies possible, with a delightful endowment of Irish
wit ; but there was to her mind certainly nobody who was

in the least her equal in her way.   There are some people
who never get any credit for what is good in them, and
some who get too much credit.   My friend was one of
those who are never done justice to, and indeed, if one
may say it, did not deserve to be done justice to, if such
a contradiction were ever true.   She thought or said that
she had been more than done justice to in the former
part of her life,—that she had been admired, followed,
and adored with more than her share of devotion; and
indeed this might have been quite true, for she must
have been beautiful when she was young, and full of a
sparkle of wit and cleverness and accomplishments.   But
certainly there was very little of this in the latter part
of her life, though she was still a pretty woman at forty-
five, and infinitely superior to many of those who had
no good word for her.   It might be because she was
abandoned by her fine friends, or it might be that she
found something sympathetic in me, who have always
been a very good listener, and apt to admire and be
interested in attractive people, but she fell into a great
intimacy with me, and used to spend at least half of
her time in my house.   I believed at first, of course,
all she told me of the unkindness of others: some of it
was true; some of it, it became apparent in the course
of years, was not true, or at least not all true, though
probably she was not aware of this, and took her own
part always with a zeal and vehemence which made
her feel everybody else more completely in the wrong
than it is safe to believe everybody who is against
one can be.   She had not the merry heart which goes
all the way, the happy blood that Mrs Craven speaks
of; and yet she had a certain version of the merry
heart, and threw herself into all the little entertainments
and pleasures which I gradually began to be drawn
into, by reason of the household of girls I soon had.
Cousin Annie, whom I did not know before, drifted towards me almost as soon as I came to Windsor, and as
she was an orphan without a home, stayed with me for a

number of years; and Sara and Fanny Tulloch paid me
long visits; and my boys began to spring up and carried
me along on the stream of their rising life. My neighbour threw herself into all we did, and we soon began
to do a great deal. It makes me wonder, looking back,
how, after the despair of my grief, which found so much
utterance, I should have risen again into absolute gaiety
thus, twice over. But so it was. I thought it was for
the young people round me, and no doubt it was so, but
equally without doubt my own life burst forth again
with an obstinate elasticity which I could not keep
down. The merry heart goes all the way. I worked
very hard all the time, but could always spare a day
or any amount of evenings to please the girls, still
more to please the boys. For the children, after my
Cyril went to Eton, we began to have theatricals, which
grew into more and more importance, till we used to
play Shakespeare and Molière in my little drawing-room,
alternating with innocent versions of "Barbe Bleue,"
&c., but that in the earlier days. I never attempted
any performance myself but once, that of Mrs Hardcastle in "She Stoops to Conquer." Of course the great
inspiration of these performances was Mr Frank Tarver,
an Eton master, an excellent amateur actor, who, as
he very soon fell in love with Sara, made himself prime
minister, or, at least, master of the revels, with great
energy, and helped to keep up the circle of amusement.
There were others, too, full of character, and as interesting in their way as if they had been great lights in
the literary or any other world, whom I might describe,
and who made up a very intelligent and light-hearted
society; but as not one of them turned out remarkable
in any way, I need not insist upon them. One, who
was one of the first to break the circle, my young friend
Captain Gun, an engineer officer stationed here, I may
mention. He was the Tony to my Mrs Hardcastle,—a
large plain young man, full of ability and force. Had
he lived he would no doubt, have come to something.

He had the readiness and resource of a soldier, seeing in a moment in a way that seemed magic to me where there was any kind of danger. I remember in Romney lock, in the dusk of a summer night, a sudden incomprehensible movement of his which filled me with alarm for a moment, as he suddenly made a step out of our boat, which shivered with the motion, into another close by and dimly seen. He had perceived that it was in unskilful hands, and that the bow had caught in the side of the lock,—a dangerous position, which his sudden additional weight at once remedied. This to my ignorance was wonderful, though, of course, it was the simplest thing in the world; but the quick sight and the quick action were delightful to witness, as soon as one understood them. Captain Gun married a few years later a lady wonderfully like Fanny, who died soon, and he died shortly after, on which last occasion there were some very curious incidents took place with the table-rapping, to which we had given ourselves, with much levity, for the moment,—the only serious experience we ever had.

Into the midst of this half-childish gaiety there came a very sudden and alarming interruption. My brother Frank had married at the same time as I myself did, and had lived a very humdrum but happyish life with a wife who suited him, and had now four children—a boy and three girls. He had been in rather delicate health for a year or two, and had fallen into rather a nervous condition, his hand shaking very much so that it was difficult for him to write, though he still could do his work. For this reason I heard from them rarely, as Jeanie, his wife, was a bad correspondent too. One morning very suddenly, and in the most painful and disagreeable way, I heard that he had got into great trouble about money, and was, in fact, a ruined man. It was the thunderbolt out of the clear sky, which is always so tremendous. I spent a day of misery, expecting him to come to me, not knowing what to expect, and fearing all sorts of things. A day or two after I went

to look for him, and found him absent and his wife in
great trouble. His health, from what I now heard, was
altogether shattered; and it was that as much as anything
else which had brought his affairs into the most hopeless
muddle, from which there seemed no escape. They
had not very much money at any time, but what they
had had somehow slipped through his fingers. His wife
and I did everything we could, but that was very little.
He was a man without an expensive taste, the most
innocent, the most domestic of men, but what he had
had always slipped through his fingers, as I well knew.
Poor dear Frank! how well I remembered the use he
made of one of my mother's Scotch proverbs to justify
some new small expense following a bigger one which
he would allow to be imprudent. "Well," he would say,
half-coaxing, half-apologetic, "what's the use of eating
the coo and worrying [choking] on her tail?" Alas!
he had choked on the tail this time without remedy,
and the only thing to be done was to wind up the
affairs as well as was possible, and to further the little
family, whom he could not live without, after him,
which was what we did accordingly, with a prompt
action which was some relief to our heavy hearts. We
neither of us had a word of blame on our lips or a
thought of anger in our hearts. Frank and Nelly, the
two elder children, came to me, and Jeanie with her
two little girls (my two girls this many a year, and
now the only comfort of my life) joined her husband
in France. It was a terrible break in life, and affected
me in many ways permanently; but after the shock of
seeing that chasm opening at our feet, and all their life
shattered to pieces, everything quieted down again. The
children were well. Oh, magic of life that made everything go smooth! they had taken no harm. They had
their lives before them, and unbounded possibilities of
making everything right. I am not sure that I had not
a sort of secret satisfaction in getting Frank, my nephew,
into my hands, thinking, with that complacency with

which we always look at our own doings, that I could
now train him for something better than they had
thought of. This was in 1868. My Cyril was twelve
and at Eton, having his room at his tutor's, and living
precisely like other Eton boys, though coming home to
sleep, which was one of the greatest happinesses in
my life. Frank was fourteen, a big strong boy. I
planned to send him to Eton too, but coming home
for his meals, which was much less expensive, as I
could not afford the other for him, and it answered very
well. He was always the best of boys, manful, and a
steady worker. Cyril had begun to be by this time
noted as one of the cleverest boys, far on for his age,
and promising everything, besides the brightest, wittiest,
most sparkling little fellow, as he always was. I used
to make it my boast that both my boys received Frank
as a true brother, and never would have allowed me,
had I wished it, to give them any pleasure or advantage
which he did not share. Nelly after a while went to
her mother's sister, Mrs Sime, and so we all settled
down. But it is not likely that such family details would
be of interest to the public.

And yet, as a matter of fact, it is exactly those family
details that are interesting,—the human story in all its
chapters. I have often said, however, that none of us
with any of the strong sense of family credit which used
to be so general, but is not so, I think, now, could ever
really tell what were perhaps the best and most creditable
things in our own life, since by the strange fate which
attends us human creatures, what is most creditable to
one is often least creditable to another. These things
steal out ; they are divined in most cases, and then forgotten. Therefore all can never be told of any family
story, except at the cost of family honour, and that pride
which is the most pardonable of all pride, the determination to keep unsullied a family name. This catastrophe
was tremendous in appearance, and yet was more or less
a good thing for the children, whose prospects seemed to

be utterly ruined,—not for the parents. Poor Jeanie—
not strong enough, I suppose, to bear what fell upon her,
as she had not been strong enough to do anything to
prevent it—died most unexpectedly in her sleep, in a mild
attack of fever which excited no alarm. My brother had
been glad to get an appointment among the employees
of a railway that was being made, of all places in the
world, in Hungary, and went there with his wife and
the little girls. I forget how long they were there,—only
a very short time. The shock of their downfall was over,
they were more or less happy to be together, and Frank
and Nelly were happy enough here. We had returned
to all our little gaieties again, our theatricals,—our boating, and the rest,—without much thought on my part,
I fear, of the additional responsibility I had upon me
of another boy to educate and set out in the world. We
were all assembled, a merry party enough, one summer
evening, after an afternoon on the river, at a late meal,
—a sort of supper,—when a telegram was put into my
hand. I remember the look of the long table and
all the bright faces round it, the pretty summer dishes,
salad, and pink salmon, and ornamented sweet things,
and many flowers, the men and boys in their flannels,
the girls in their light summer dresses,—everything light
and bright. I have often said that it was the only telegram I ever received without a certain tremor of anxiety.
Captain Gun, who was there, had been uncertain of his
coming on this particular day, and a good many telegrams
on that subject had been passing between us. I held the
thing in my hand and looked across at him, and said,
"This time it cannot be from you." Then I opened it
with the laugh in my mouth, and this is what I read:
"Jeanie is dead, and I am in despair." It was like a
scene in a tragedy. They all saw the change in my face,
but I dreaded to say anything, for there was her son
sitting by, my good Frank, as gay as possible. He was
only about fifteen, or perhaps sixteen. We managed to
keep it from him till next morning, not to give him that

shock in the midst of his pleasure; and somehow the supper got completed without any one knowing what had happened.

A very short time after my poor brother came home with the two little white-faced, forlorn children, with their big eyes. I never thought but that it must kill him, but it did not; though, when I met them at Victoria, I thought I never should have got him safely back, even to Windsor. He was completely shattered, like a man in a palsy, for a time scarcely able to stand or to speak, but not so overwhelmed with grief as I expected. Grief is the strangest thing, or rather it is very wonderful in how many different ways people take those blows, which from outside seem as if they must be final. Especially is it so in the closest of human connections, that between man and wife. People who have seemed to be all the world to each other are parted so, and the survivor, who is for the moment as my poor brother said "in despair," shows the most robust power of bearing it, and is so soon himself or herself again, that one, confounded and half-ashamed, feels that one is half-ridiculous to have expected anything different. Frank, poor fellow, had got over his sorrow on the long journey. He came to me like a child glad to get home, not much disturbed about anything that could happen. He lived for about six years after, for a great part of the time in tolerable comfort, but, so far as work was concerned, was capable of no more. The shaking of his hand was never cured, nor even sufficiently improved to make writing of any kind possible. He settled down to a kind of quiet life, read his newspaper, took his walk, sat in his easy-chair in the dining-room or in his own room for the rest of the day, was pleased with Frank's progress and with Nelly's love for reading, and with his little girls, and so got through his life, I think, not unhappily. But he and I, who had been so much to each other once, were nothing to each other now. I sometimes thought he looked at me as a kind of stepmother to his children, and we no longer thought alike on almost any subject: he had drifted one way and I another. He did not even take very much interest in me, and I fear he often irritated me. Poor Frank! it was sometimes a great trial, and I often wonder how the life went on, on the whole, so well as it did. He entertained delusive hopes for a time of going back and of being able to do something; but they were evidently from the first delusions and nothing more, and it did not hurt him so much as might have been thought when they vanished,—he had too little strength to feel it, I suppose.

Of course I had to face a prospect considerably changed by this great addition to my family. I had been obliged to work pretty hard before to meet all the too great expenses of the house. Now four people were added to it, very small two of them, but the others not inexpensive members of the house. I remember making a kind of pretence to myself that I had to think it over, to make a great decision, to give up what hopes I might have had of doing now my very best, and to set myself steadily to make as much money as I could, and do the best I could for the three boys. I think that in some pages of my old book I have put this down with a little half-sincere attempt at a heroical attitude. I don't think, however, that there was any reality in it. I never did nor could, of course, hesitate for a moment as to what had to be done. It had to be done, and that was enough, and there is no doubt that it was much more congenial to me to drive on and keep everything going, with a certain scorn of the increased work, and metaphorical toss of my head, as if it mattered! than it ever would have been to labour with an artist's fervour and concentration to produce a masterpiece. One can't be two things or serve two masters. Which was God and which was mammon in that individual case it would be hard to say, perhaps; for once in a way mammon, meaning the money which fed my flock, was in a kind of a poor way God, so far as the necessities of that crisis went. And the wonder was that we did it, I can't tell how, economising, I fear, very little, never knowing quite at the beginning of the year how the ends would come together at Christmas, always with troublesome debts and forestalling of money earned, so that I had generally eaten up the price of a book before it was printed, but always—thank God for it !—so far successfully that, though always owing somebody, I never owed anybody to any unreasonable amount or for any unreasonable extent of time, but managed to pay everything and do everything, to stint nothing, to give them all that was happy and pleasant and of good report through all those dear and blessed boyish years. I confess that it was not done in the noblest way, with those strong efforts of self-control and economy which some people can exercise. I could not do that, or at least did not, but I could work. And I did work, joyfully, with pleasure in it and in my life, sometimes with awful moments when I did not know how I should ever pass some dreadful corner, where the way seemed to end and the rocks to close in : but the corner was always rounded, the road opened up again.

I recollect one of these moments especially, I forget the date : I always do forget dates, but the circumstances were these. We were a family of eight, children included, two boys at Eton, almost always guests in the house,—every kind of thing (in our modest way) going on, small dinner-parties, and a number of mild amusements, when it so happened that I came to a pause and found that every channel was closed and no place for any important work. I had always a lightly flowing stream of magazine articles, &c., and refused no work that was offered to me ; but the course of life could not have been carried on on these, and a large sum was wanted at brief intervals to clear the way. I had, I think, a novel written, but did not know where I should find a place for it. Literary business arrangements were not organised then as now—there was no such thing as a literary agent. Serials in magazines were published in much less number, magazines themselves being not half so many (and a good thing too!). The consequence was that I seemed to be at a dead standstill. It was like nothing but what I have already said, — a mountainous road making a sharp turn round a corner, when it seems to disappear altogether, as if it ended there in the closing in of the cliffs. I was miserably anxious, not knowing where to turn or what to do, hoping every morning would bring me some proposal, waiting upon God, if I may use the word (I did the thing with the most complete faith, —what could I else?), for the opening up of that closed way. One evening I got a letter from a man whose name I did not know, asking if he could come to see me about a business matter. I forget whether he mentioned the name of the 'Graphic,' then just established,—I think not; at all events there was nothing in the letter to make me think it of any importance. I replied, however (I didn't always reply so quickly), appointing the second day after to receive him. I had decided to go to London next day to see if I could persuade some one to take my novel and give a good price for it. I think it was to Mr George Smith I went, who was very kind and gracious, as was his wont, but would have nothing to say to me. I fancy I went somewhere else, but I had no success. I recollect coming home in a kind of despair, and being met at the door when it was opened to me by the murmur of the merry house, the cheerful voices, the overflowing home, — every corner full and warm as if it had a steady income and secure revenue at its back. My brother, I remember, who I suppose had seen some cloud on my face before I left, came forward to meet me with some trivial question, hoping I had not felt cold or taken cold or something, which in the state of despair in which I was had a sort of exasperating effect upon me; but they were all dispersing over the house to get ready for dinner, and I escaped further notice. No one thought anything more than that I was dull or cross for the rest of the evening. I used to work very late then, always till two in the morning (it is past three at this moment, 18th, nay, 19th April 1895, but this is no longer usual with me). I can't remember whether I worked that night, but I think it was one of the darkest nights (oh, no, no, that I should say so! they were all safe and well), at least a very dreadful moment, and I could not think what I should do.

Next morning came my visitor. He came from the 'Graphic': he wanted a story, I think the first they had had. He wanted it very soon, the first instalments within a week or two; and after a little talk and negotiation, he came to the conclusion that they would give me £1300. The road did run round that corner after all. Our Father in heaven had settled it all the time for the children; there had never been any doubt. I was absolutely without hope or help. I did not know where to turn, and here, in a moment, all was clear again—the road free in the sunshine, the cloud in a moment rolled away.

It was not, however, the story which I had finished at the time which I gave them (which did not seem suitable). I began another instantly, and went on with it in instalments, I think. It was the novel called 'Innocent,' and was not very good, so far as I can remember, though the idea was one that had pleased me,—the development by successive shocks of feeling of a girl of dormant intelligence. I believe the trial scene in it was very badly managed—not unnatural, for I never was present at a trial, though that, of course, was no excuse. It was seldom that an incident so dramatic as this little episode I have described took place in my life; but it was checkered with similar, if lesser, crises. It was always a struggle to get safely through every year and make my ends meet. Indeed I fear they never did quite meet; there was always a tugging together, which cost me a great deal of work and much anxiety. The wonder was that the much was never too much. I always managed it somehow, thank God! very happy (and presuming a little on my privilege) when I saw the way tolerably clear before me, and knew at the beginning of the year where the year's income was to come from, but driving, ploughing on, when I was not at all sure of that all the same, and in some miraculous way getting through. If I had not had unbroken health, and a spirit almost criminally elastic, I could not have done it. I ought to have been worn out by work, and crushed by care, half a hundred times by all rules, but I never was so. Good day and ill day, they balanced each other, and I got on through year after year. This, I am afraid, sounds very much like a boast. (I was going to add, "but I don't mean it as such.") I am not very sure, however, that I don't mean it, or that my head might not be a little turned sometimes by a sense of the rashness and dare-devilness, if I may use such a word, of my own proceedings; and it was in its way an immoral, or at least an un-moral, mode of life, dashing forward in the face of all obstacles and taking up all burdens with a kind of levity, as if my strength and resource could never fail. If they had failed, I should have been left in the direst bankruptcy; and I had no right to reckon upon being always delivered at the critical moment. I should think any one who did so blamable now. I persuaded myself then that I could not help it, that no better way was practicable, and indeed did live by faith, whether it was or was not exercised in a legitimate way. I might say now that another woman doing the same thing was tempting Providence. To tempt Providence or to trust God, which was it? In my own case, naturally, I said the latter, and did not in the least deserve, in my temerity, to be led and constantly rescued as I was. I must add that I never had any help from outside. I never received so much as a legacy in my life. My publishers were good and kind in the way of making me advances, without which I could not have got on; but they were never—probably because of these advances, and of my constant need and inability, both by circumstances and nature, to struggle over prices—very lavish in payment. Still, I made on

I

the whole a large income — and spent it, taking no thought of the morrow. Yes, taking a great deal of thought of the morrow in the way of constant work and constant undertaking of whatever kind of work came to my hand. But, indeed, I do not defend myself. It would have been better if I could have added the grace of thrift, which is said to be the inheritance of the Scot, to the faculty of work. I feel that I leave a very bad lesson behind me; but I am afraid that the immense relief of getting over a crisis gave a kind of reflected enjoyment to the trouble between, and that these alternations of anxiety and deliverance were more congenial than the steady monotony of self-denial, not to say that the still better kind of self-denial which should have made a truer artist than myself pursue the higher objects of art, instead of the mere necessities of living, was wanting too. I pay the penalty in that I shall not leave anything behind me that will live. What does it matter? Nothing at all now—never anything to speak of. At my most ambitious of times I would rather my children had remembered me as their mother than in any other way, and my friends as their friend. I never cared for anything else. And now that there are no children to whom to leave any memory, and the friends drop day by day, what is the reputation of a circulating library to me? Nothing, and less than nothing—a thing the thought of which now makes me angry, that any one should for a moment imagine I cared for that, or that it made up for any loss. I am perhaps angry, less reasonably, when well-intentioned people tell me I have done good, or pious ones console me for being left behind by thoughts of the good I must yet be intended to do. God help us all! what is the good done by any such work as mine, or even better than mine? "If any man build upon this foundation . . . wood, hay, stubble; . . . if the work shall be burned, he shall suffer loss: but he himself shall be saved; yet so as by fire." An infinitude of pains and labour, and all to disappear like the stubble and the hay.

Yet who knows? The little faculty may grow a bigger one in the more genial land to come, where one will have no need to think of the boiling of the daily pot. In the meantime it was good to have kept the pot boiling and maintained the cheerful household fire so long, though it is smouldering out in darkness now.

There is one thing, however, I have always whimsically resented, and that is the contemptuous compliments that for many years were the right thing to address to me and to say of me, as to my "industry." Now that I am old the world is a little more respectful, and I have not heard so much about my industry for some time. The delightful superiority of it in the mouth of people who had neither industry nor anything else to boast of used to make me very wroth, I avow,—wroth with a laugh and rueful half sense of the justice of it in the abstract, though not from those who spoke. The same kind of feeling made me angry the other day even, comically, not seriously angry, at a bit of a young person who complimented me on my 'Beleaguered City.' Now, I am quite willing that people like Mr Hutton should speak of the 'Beleaguered City' as of the one little thing among my productions that is worth remembering (no, Mr Hutton does nothing of the kind—he is not that kind of person), but I felt inclined to say to the other, "The 'Beleaguered City,' indeed, my young woman! I should think something a good deal less than that might be good enough for you." By which it may perhaps be suspected that I don't always think such small beer of myself as I say, but this is a pure matter of comparison.

I need scarcely say that there was not much of what one might call a literary life in all this. I was very seldom in town, Windsor being near enough to permit of almost all that one wanted to do in town, except society, being done in a day, between two trains so to speak, which was the most convenient thing in the world, and the most impossible for any sort of social intercourse. Even a dinner - party, which could only

be done at the cost of a visit, thus became much more
out of the question than if I had lived at a greater
distance, and thus been compelled to pass a week or
two occasionally in London. Now and then I went
to a luncheon-party or an afternoon gathering, both of
which things I detested. Curiously enough, being fond
on the whole of my fellow-creatures, I always disliked
paying visits, and felt myself a fish out of water when
I was not in my own house, — not to say that I was
constantly wanted at home, and proud to feel that I
was so. The work answered very well for a pretence
to get me off engagements, but I could always have
managed the work if I had liked the pleasure, or supposed pleasure. I need not speak, however, as if I had
been a person in much request, which would be giving
an entirely false view of myself. I never was so in the
least. From the days when my Jewish friend com-
plained that I did not do myself justice, with the
aggrieved tone of a woman to whom I had thus done
a great injustice by not doing anything to make myself
agreeable or remarkable, being asked to her house for
that purpose, I have always been a disappointment to
my friends. I have no gift of talk, not much to say;
and though I have always been an excellent listener,
that only succeeds under auspicious circumstances.

I think I never met so many people as in the days of
Mrs Duncan Stewart, that dear and bright old lady who
used to fill her little rooms in Sloane Street with the
most curious jumble of entertaining people and people
who came to be entertained, the smartest (odious word!)
of society, and all the luminaries of the moment, many
writers, artists, &c., and a few mountebanks to make up.
She herself was very worthy of a place in any picture-gal-
lery. There is a very droll sketch of her by Mr Augustus
Hare, which does no justice to the subject. She was an
English and nineteenth-century shadow of the French
ladies who take up so much space in the records of the
eighteenth, and who were, indeed, I suppose, of no more

personal consequence than she, were it not for the mention they have secured in so many records of a memoir-
writing time, and the numbers of great people who circled
round them.   Mrs Stewart had known almost everybody
in her day, which of itself is a wonderful attraction.   She
had at one time seen much of Disraeli—almost at one
time run the risk of having her head turned by him.
The loves (but this never came to be a love—on her side
at least; "For, my dear," she used to say, "I had the
great preservation of being in love with my husband")
of a lady of eighty are always amusing and pathetic.
Age takes all the doubtfulness out of them, and gives
them a piquancy as of the loves of children.   She had
ancient suitors, worshippers of her old age, always about
her.   I believe she refused a proposal of marriage after
she was seventy.   She was at the time I knew her of the
most picturesque appearance, with a delicate small face
of the colour of ivory, fine features, except that always
troublesome mouth, which is imperfect in almost every
face that is good for anything, and those dim blue eyes
which have a charm of their own—half veiled and mystic.
She was one of those people who do not grow grey, and
she wore a peculiar head-dress—a kerchief of fine muslin
and lace falling upon her shoulders, and softly veiling her
small erect head.   In the middle of the flutter of general
company about her, she had always (as indeed every one
has) a constant circle of intimates always the same, and
sometimes not quite worthy of the idol they surrounded.
It seems a law of nature that this should be so, and that
every remarkable person should have a little ring of commonplace satellites, who are apt to make the object of
their adoration a little absurd, out of pure love and desire
to do her or him honour, with perhaps the leaven of a
little hope to do themselves honour too, by being known
as her or his friends.   This delightful old lady was very
fond of seeing and knowing everything.   She went to every
entertainment, grave or gay, and was all agog to go to
the Greek play at Eton, where it came to entrance us

from Oxford, with a chorus *pour rire* of a dozen dreadfully recognisable young Dons and scholars *affublés* in inconvenient robes and beards; as well as to see Sarah Bernhardt, or any and every novelty that turned up. "La pièce m'interesse," she said, looking out upon her parties with her dim eyes that saw everything, and never so pleased as when the crowd fluttered about her, and a little special court gathered round her sofa. Some vile young journalist, I remember, made a cruel sketch of her, which was published in a cruel and wicked series then giving great piquancy to the 'Saturday Review' (I think it was in the Girl of the Period and Mature Siren time, which are all so forgotten nowadays), for which I hope he has had his deserts somewhere. Of course, nothing could be easier than to travesty this sweet and bright old lady into a spectre of society, clinging on to the last to social dissipations, and incapable of being alone — and nothing more absolutely untrue. Her grandchild said of her after she was dead, in the hush of that pause in which the longing to know what they are doing, what they are thinking who have left us, is overwhelming, "Oh, she will have no time to think of us, she will be so much interested in seeing everything." Even in the shock of loss it was impossible not to be consoled by the thought of that vivid curiosity and interest and enjoyment with which she would find a new sphere before her, with everything to be found out.

Whom did I meet at Mrs Stewart's? I forget; nobody, I suppose, of any great consequence. She had little boxes of rooms over a tailor's shop in Sloane Street, and there gave the most elaborate luncheons, all sorts of delicacies, to which a number of very fine people would crowd in, sitting at all the uneasy angles of a table with adjuncts to it, which completely filled the room. Her income, I believe, was as small as her rooms; and her pleasant way was to tell her daughter or some intimate friend she had so many people coming to lunch, and then to prepare her pretty head-dress

and her careful little *mise en scène* to receive them, with
no further thought of more substantial preparations.
But the table groaned all the same, and there was
every costly and delicate viand on it that was to be
had, and heaps of flowers, thanks always to her
daughter or her loving admirers.   There used to be
Lady Martin often, in a large Rubens hat and long
sweeping feather, though long past the age of such
vanities, seventy or thereabouts, with all the old world
graces, and the consciousness of having been more admired than any woman of her day, which gives an ineffable air to an old beauty.   Her husband, the excellent
Sir Theodore, was so evidently and so constantly the first
of all her admirers, leading the band, that the group was
always interesting and touching in its bygoneness yet
perfect sincerity and good faith.   She wrote her book
after this about the Shakespeare parts she had played,—
that strange, elegant, antiquated expression of the graceful feminine enthusiast accustomed to applause which,
at least in the case of a good woman, at her age is so
touching as to make one ashamed of the smile which
fades away almost into sentiment while we look on
and are ashamed of ourselves.   There was the twinkle
of Bon Gaultier in Sir Theodore's eye on other matters,
but never where his wife was concerned.   And a very
frequent visitor was the kind, the gentle, the sympathetic Censor of Plays, dead only this year, Mr Pigott,
a man to whom everybody's heart went out, I don't
know exactly why or how, except from an intuition of
friendship, a sort of instinct.   He was always interested, always kind,—a sort of atmosphere of humanity
and warm feeling and sympathy about him, his little
round form and round head radiating warmth and kindliness.   He is the only man I have ever met, I think,
from whom I never heard an unkind word of any one.
This, to tell the sad truth, is apt to make conversation
a little insipid; but he had the most extensive acquaintance both with people and things, and had many a

happy turn of expression and *mot* of social wisdom which preserved him from that worst of faults : he was never dull, though always kind, which is almost a paradox. I have my own way of dividing people, as I suppose most of us have. There are those whom I can talk to, and those whom I can't. With the first no subject is needed, the conversation goes on of itself; with the other all the finest subjects in the world produce no result. (I remember as I write one story of Mr Pigott which slightly, but very slightly, contradicts this statement that he never said an unkind word. We were talking once of the son - in - law of a friend of ours, who had most gratuitously and unnecessarily appeared against her in a trial in which she was unhappily involved, to prove (as if any one could prove such a thing) that certain anonymous letters were written by her. We were discussing his conduct with indignation, when Mr Pigott looked up with a smile,—" Look in his face and you'll forgive him all," he said. It was true that the man was a fool, and bore it on his face.)

It was with Mrs Stewart that I first saw Tennyson. She had, I suppose, asked leave to take me there with her to luncheon, and I was of course glad to go, though a little unwilling, as my manner was. I forget where it was — an ordinary London house, where they were living for the season. Mrs Tennyson lay upon her sofa, as she did always — though able to be taken to the luncheon-table by her excellent son Hallam, whom I knew a little, and who was always kind and pleasant. I have always thought that Tennyson's appearance was too emphatically that of a poet, especially in his photographs : the fine frenzy, the careless picturesqueness, were almost too much. He looked the part too well; but in reality there was a roughness and acrid gloom about the man which saved him from his over romantic appearance. He paid no attention to me, as was very natural. The conversation turned somehow

upon his little play of "The Falcon"—now more forgotten, I think, than any of his others, though it seemed
to me much the most effective of them. I said something about its beauty, and that I thought it just the
kind of entertainment which a gracious prince might
offer to his guests; and he replied, with a sort of indignant sense of grievance, "And they tell me people
won't go to see it." I am afraid, however, that I did
not attract the poet in any way, to Mrs Stewart's great
disappointment and annoyance. She was eager to point
out to me that he was much occupied by a very old
lady — a fair, little, white-haired woman, nearly eighty,
the mother of Mr Tom Hughes (Tom Brown), who
was just then going out to America to the settlement
in the backwoods which was called Rugby, in Tennes-
see, where the young Hughes were, and which was
going to be the most perfect colony on the face of
the earth, filled with nothing but the cardinal virtues.
I think the old lady died there, and I know the settlement went sadly to pieces and ruined many hopes.
However, feeling I had not been entirely a success,—a
feeling very habitual to me,—I was glad of Mrs Stewart's
sign of departure, and went up to Mrs Tennyson on
the sofa, to which she had returned, to take my leave.
I am never good at parting politenesses, and I daresay
was very *gauche* in saying that it was so kind of her
to ask me; while she graciously responded that she
was delighted to have seen me, &c., according to the
established ritual in such cases. Tennyson was standing by, lowering over us with his ragged beard and his
saturnine look. He eyed us, while these pretty speeches
were being made, with cynical eyes. "What liars you
women are!" he said. There could not have been anything more true; but, to be sure, it was not so civil as
it was true. I never saw him again till that recent
occasion when my Cecco and I went to Farringford
when he was Lord Tennyson, and very old and infirm,
and his wife was a shrunken old, old lady, laid upon

a sofa from which she never moved, the flood of life flowing past her but never touching her,—a pathetic sight.
It was after Lionel's death, and after my Cyril's death,
and· I sat by her and cried; but she seemed in her
old age as if she could weep no more. That time
Lord Tennyson was delightful—kind and friendly and
full of stories, talking a great deal, and in the best of
humours. He read the " Funeral Ode " to us afterwards, and one or two shorter poems ("Blow, bugles,
blow "); and I was so glad and thankful that Cecco
should see him so, and have such a bright recollection
of him to carry through his life. Alas! alas! It had
always been a regret that he had never seen Carlyle—
so little as it matters now!

It is rather a fictitious sort of thing recalling those
semi-professional recollections. It is by way of a kind
of apology for knowing so few notable people. I met
Mr Fawcett once, the blind politician, a huge mild man,
cheerful in talk and amiable in countenance, whom somebody (not me, I am afraid) overheard saying to his wife
when she came back to him from another room, to take—
the small smiling woman she was—his colossal person in
charge, " Oh, Milly, your step is like music." He spoke
to me very kindly, magnifying my work, though I don't
remember how, except the pleasant impression. At the
same party was Sir Charles Dilke, who, on being introduced to me, began at once to speak of *his* books and of
his publishers, as if he and not I were the literary person.
The same thing happened with a great lady I afterwards
met in the same house,—a Roman Catholic lady, and
a very great personage. There had been several invitations given to her at one time and another by the
mistress of the house, but they all failed somehow, and
at last the one she could accept fell on a Friday. The
great lady took the trouble to write the day before to
remind my friend that it *was* Friday, and consequently
to her a fast day. This put C. R. on her mettle, as any

one who knows her will understand, and we were served
with the most exquisite and luxurious meal, I don't know
how many *maigre* dishes—fish, eggs, and vegetables, all
beautifully cooked and seductive to the last degree, about
as little like fasting as the imagination could conceive.
I like fish and vegetables better than any other kind of
food, and, beguiled by the variety, followed Lady ———'s
example and kept up with her as long as I could. But it
was a vain attempt, and I had to sit and look on for some
time while she travelled valiantly through every dish.
She, too, chose as the theme of her conversation her
own books, their success or rather their relative successes,
and the troubles she had with her publishers, and all the
rest, while I sat with rueful amusement listening, feeling
my little *rôle* taken from me. The worst was, I had
never heard she had written anything, and was in mortal
terror of betraying my ignorance! What with her literature, and her beautiful appetite, and our beautiful meal,
the occasion was delightful. There were some actor-
gentlemen of the party,—I know not if the great lady had
a liking for actors, but there they were, furtively regaled
with beef after the lighter quips and fancies of the feast,
and rather ignored in consequence by us finer people who
had fasted on about twenty of the daintiest dishes in the
world.

The year 1875 was an era in my life—a great many
things happened in that year. Frank, my good Frank,
my nephew, who had grown the most trustworthy and
satisfactory boy in the world, loving home, fond of
amusement and diversion, but only in the right ways,
—such a one as is a stand-by and tower of strength in a
family,—completed his work at Cooper's Hill very well,
taking a high place, and so having the right to choose
what part of India he would go to. Things had so
developed in the family that this event seemed an
occasion for various other changes, especially as at
the same time Cyril was to go to Oxford. My brother

had been getting feeble and less easy to take care of,
and I was anxious that he should live in a doctor's house
and be watched and cared for, as his state seemed to
demand; and he was himself desirous of making a
change, although his plan for himself was quite different,
and he preferred the freedom of going off by himself
somewhere as my father had done, and living in his
own way, for which he was evidently not strong enough,
though he did not perceive it himself. We settled, however, that when the elder boys, as we called them, went
away, Frank to India and Cyril to Balliol, this further
move should be decided on; and that the little girls,
whose education ought to be seriously thought of, should
go to Germany at the same time. I think the pressure
of my poor brother's illness, though he was not ill then
but only ailing, and of his different way of looking at
things and perhaps unconscious criticism and often dis-
approval of my ways, had become a little too much for
me, and he wanted to be free himself, and when his
children were gone would no longer have had anything
to bind him to my house. But all this was made unnecessary, these plans and arrangements, as often happens
in such a breaking up. Death is often opportune, as
Mr Pigott said. I was trying to make Frank's last
summer at home pleasant, and wanted him within the
limitations of our small ways to see and do everything
possible. There is an incident in one of my own
books, in ' Kirsteen,' which is a sort of illustration of
my feeling about him. It was not my own invention,
but told me as the family custom in the large, poor,
proud family which formed the model of the family
in that book,—the bottle of champagne solemnly produced and drunk by the whole party on the night
before the boy went away. I wanted Frank to have
his bottle of champagne. I had settled to take them
all to Switzerland for one thing, and I took them up
to an opera for another, and to stay a night or two in

London, and to see everything they could see in the small amount of time. There was a match going on at Lord's, I think, which filled the morning, and then we were to dine at Miss Blackwood's, and stay in the same house in Half Moon Street where she was. All was very lively and pleasant for the boys, who went up in the morning all so bright and gay, with their little bows of blue ribbon, and button-holes with a bit of forget-me-not, to serve the same purpose. How often have I come out with them to the door, seeing them off, so spruce, in the bright morning (surely the days were always bright when they went up for that Eton and Harrow match), so full of pleasure. I found one of these little blue bows in my Cyril's room after—God bless him!—and it lies with other treasures. I can see them now setting out, the little hall full of the little bustle, and I half scolding, telling them they were sure to be late, and so proud—the three of them—all well, not a cloud, the most hopeful youths, Frank tall and strong, my Cyril with his beautiful face, my Cecco only a boy and little, straining to keep up with them, all dressed in their best, with that keen regard to the fashion which I laughed at and loved, — but what did I not love in them? They were my all in this world. I was always anxious; but there was not a cloud upon the skies, and what had I to fear?

Next morning we were called back by a telegram. My brother had been taken ill, and the little scheme of pleasure was broken up. I found him very ill, scarcely conscious, when I got home, and in that state he remained, with a few lightenings, till he died. It lasted only a few days. He was not quite sixty, but worn out, and his life withered away to the barest skeleton of living. Often, often have I been vexed with thoughts that I might have been more tender to him. I did all I could for him, grudging nothing, but we had veered far away from each other, and I do not know that I was always kind. But it was not in unkindness, but with a full heart, that I thanked God for his release then. He was taken away from the partings which would have been hard to bear, from the evil to come: he had not to give up his son or to part with his little girls; and I was glad for him. He was delivered just in time, and slept and dreamed away, without any trouble in going so far as any one knew. He had not taken very much part in our life; the children, who were much with him, were too young to mourn except for the moment.

There was one thing that it was a balm to me to think of. At first it was supposed that he might rally and go on for some time, for two years perhaps, the doctor said. I took my own boys into council, and they both said warmly, with all their hearts, that there must be no thought now of any change,—that we could let him go into no stranger's hands now that he was ill. It cost my Cecco something to make such resolutions as that, I knew after, but only long after. To Cyril it cost nothing, but they both agreed cordially, both the boys, as to a thing that could not be gainsaid. But they were not put to the proof—and he was saved seeing them all go away.

Cyril left Eton at the end of that half, a little while after. When he went down to see if the lists were out before we left home, the man at Drakes told him, smiling, that he could not tell him the names, but he could tell him this, that in the first three, two were Oppidans. This was very rare, and there was little doubt that he was one of them. He and Frank came rushing up with this exciting news to tell me. I have had great trouble, but also I have had many joys. I forget who the Colleger was who was first, — I think it was Ryle, or perhaps Harmer, now Bishop; then Farrar, Oliphant. These two went to Balliol, both with scholarships from Eton, Farrar also with a Balliol scholarship, which Cyril ought to have got too, but did not. Both of them now are, I hope and believe, fulfilling their lives in a better place than this, Farrar very young. He was more regular, more dutiful; he had not the wayward touch in him, the careless heart. He did far better after. At that time there was no better possible,—it was all triumph and anticipation of every good. Eton is very dear, very bright to me in all its recollections. No brighter being than my Cyril ever came from it, a boy unharmed in every way, handsome, winning, clever, gay, the most light-hearted, the most generous in feeling, full of understanding and of tenderness, nothing about him commonplace or dull, looking as if he would not subdue but win the whole world. I used to think that if one could desire to have another personality than one's own, his would have been the thing to dream of at that bright moment. And I used to apply to him the description of the young squire in Chaucer,

> " Singing he was, or flyting, all the day,
> He was as fresh as is the month of May."

There was no prouder woman in the world than I was with the three. Frank was twenty-two, Cyril nineteen, Cecco sixteen — he doing so well too, with his strange little ways and shyness and close clinging always to his mother. It is just twenty years ago. I think often if all had gone well, as might then have been so confidently expected,—had Frank been a prosperous man in India, perhaps sending home his children to be educated, and Cyril been a rising lawyer as was hoped, and Cecco, if delicate, still able with care to keep on,—it would all have been so natural, not anything wonderful, just the commonplace of life for which other fathers and mothers would scarcely pause to give special thanks, it being all so usual, exactly what might have been expected. And ah, the difference to me! But, thank God! we did not know what was coming in these days.

We went to Interlaken, Cecco and I and our dear
"little Nelly." The older boys took the little girls to
their German school at Arolsen, and joined us after,
coming round by the Lake of Constance. We found
Annie Thackeray, attended by Miss Huth, a gentle little
soul, very much like my little Nelly, and making great
friends with her at Interlaken; and here it was that
Annie and I became fast friends. There never was any
one more fascinating or a more delightful companion, so
pleased to please, so ready to see the best of you—a
little, perhaps, too ready to perceive a best that might
not be in you, yet with a keen observation underneath
that was—though if the report was unfavourable would
scarcely permit itself to be—critical. She was always
more effusive than myself, delightfully flattering, appreciating. I used to say that if you wanted the moon
very much, she would eagerly, and for a moment quite
seriously, think how she could help to get it for you,
scorning the bounds of the possible. We went to Grin-
delwald together and were in the same hotel—the old
Bear in its homely days — for about a fortnight, and
grew intimate. She was joined there by the Leslie
Stephens, meaning her sister Minnie and Minnie's husband. It was Mrs Stephen's last summer in this world,
but we did not know that either. She was not strong,
but there were reasons for that, and no sort of alarm
about her. Little Minnie, her one little girl, was the
baby of the party—a little, fragile, quaint thing, whom
I remember standing by the great St Bernard, Sultan,
with her hands in his deep fur, a curious little picture.
She was full of quaint sayings and wondering looks,
looking on at the boys and asking solemnly, "What are
they ninking about?" with the gravest observation, and
defending her little basket of cakes from Cyril's pretended attacks with a serious discrimination of him as
the greedy boy, which became one of our little jokes.
It takes but a small matter to make a joke when all

is well and one's heart inclined that way. I made acquaintance with Mr Leslie Stephen at that time,—a man with whom I had had a slight passage of arms by letters about some literary work, he being the editor of the 'Cornhill,' a prosperous magazine in those days. I fell into a chance talking with him one evening in front of the Bear, when the sky was growing dim over the Wetterhorn, and the shadows of the mountains drawing down as they do when night is coming on. I recollect we walked up and down and talked, I have not the smallest remembrance what about. But the end of it was that when I went in we had become friends, or so it was at least on my side.

Leslie Stephen was kind to the boys, taking them for walks with him up among the mountains; and, egged on by the ladies, he was so far kind to me that he took two of my stories for the 'Cornhill,' which meant in each case the bulk of a year's income.

This expedition was altogether very successful and delightful, the last time the three boys were to spend together, for many years, we thought,—for ever in this world, as it turned out. One thing happened in it on which I look back with a mixture of feeling and amusement. It was the coming to life of the two who were then called the little girls. They had been very unresponsive children, not "forthcoming" as Mrs Freshfield says; little shy mice, half-shy, half-defiant, as I think children often are whose childhood has been broken up by transplantation to another house. They had not had perhaps so much as they should have had of the petting of the nursery. The household when they came into it was preoccupied by the boys, who were so much older; and though everybody was kind, they missed, no doubt unconsciously, poor little souls, the something more than kindness, the indulgence, the mother. At all events they were very chilly, scared, distrustful little things. They left home with no apparent feeling at all, and much com-

K

ment among us (most of the bystanders were always rather against these two little impedimenta) at the absence of feeling. Of course they were excited by the prospect of the journey in the care of the two big brothers, and all the novelty. But when they were left in Germany among strange-speaking people, among new ways, in such a strange place, the two little hearts gushed out all at once. They wrote to me the most pathetic, imploring letters. "Oh, come and take us home; oh come, come and take us home. We will be as good as angels," said Madge, "if you will only come and take us home." It was rather hard work refusing. We were in Interlaken, I think, when these letters came, and we made up a basket of all the toys and pictures and cakes that would carry, to console them. And they soon got over their first home - sickness. And they never relapsed into those chills and mists of their childhood, but have always been since my true children, the un-questioned daughters of the house, and with no further cloud upon the completeness of their adoption—they of me, as well as I of them. The first is often the more difficult of the two.

With that year began a new life, one of which I cannot speak much. That was the burden and heat of the day: my anxieties were sometimes almost more than I could bear. I had gone through many trials, as I thought, and God knows many of them had been hard enough, but then I knew to the depths of my heart what the yoke was and how heavy. Many times I have woke in the morning feeling in myself that image of Shelley's "Prometheus," which in my youth I had vexed my husband by not appreciating, except in what seemed to me the picture rather than the poem, the man chained to the rock, with the vultures swooping down upon him. Their cruel beaks I seemed to feel in my heart the moment I awoke. Ah me, alas! pain ever, for ever, God alone knows what was the anguish of these years.

And yet now I think of *ces beaux jours quand j'étais si malheureuse*, the moments of relief were so great and so sweet that they seemed compensation for the pain,—I remembered no more the anguish. Lately in my many sad musings it has been brought very clearly before my mind how often all the horrible tension, the dread, the anxiety which there are no words strong enough to describe,—which devoured me, but which I had to conceal often behind a smiling face,—would yield in a moment, in the twinkling of an eye, at the sound of a voice, at the first look, into an ineffable ease and the overwhelming happiness of relief from pain, which is, I think, our highest human sensation, higher and more exquisite than any positive enjoyment in this world. It used to sweep over me like a wave, sometimes when I opened a door, sometimes in a letter,— in all simple ways. I cannot explain, but if this should ever come to the eye of any woman in the passion and agony of motherhood, she will more or less understand. I was thinking lately, or rather, as sometimes happens, there was suddenly presented to my mind, like a suggestion from some one else, the recollection of these ineffable happinesses, and it seemed to me that it meant that which would be when one pushed through that last door and was met—oh, by what, by whom?—by instant relief. The wave of sudden ease and warmth and peace and joy. I felt, to tell the truth, that it was one of them who brought that to my mind, and I said to myself, "I will not want any explanation, I will not ask any question,—the first touch, the first look, will be enough, as of old, yet better than of old."

I do injustice to those whom I love above all things by speaking thus, and yet what can I say? My dearest, bright, delightful boy missed somehow his footing, how can I tell how? I often think that I had to do with it, as well as what people call inherited tendencies, and, alas! the perversity of youth, which he never outgrew.

He had done everything too easily in the beginning of
his boyish career, by natural impulse and that kind of
genius which is so often deceptive in youth, and when
he came to that stage in which hard work was necessary against the competition of the hard working, he
could not believe how much more effort was necessary.
Notwithstanding all distractions he took a second-class
at Oxford,—a great disappointment, yet not disgraceful
after all. And I will not say that, except at the first
keen moment of pain, I was in any way bitterly disappointed. *Tout peut se réparer.* I always felt so to
the end, and perhaps he thought I took it lightly, and
that it did not so much matter. Then it was one of
my foolish ways to take my own work very lightly,
and not to let them know how hard pressed I was
sometimes, so that he never, I am sure, was convinced
how serious it was in that way, and certainly never
was convinced that he could not, when the moment
came, right himself and recover lost way. But only
the moment, God bless him! did not come till God
took it in His own hands. Another theory I have thought
of with many tears lately. I had another foolish way
of laughing at the superior people, the people who took
themselves too seriously,—the boys of pretension, and all
the strong intellectualisms. This gave him, perhaps, or
helped him to form, a prejudice against the good and
reading men, who have so many affectations, poor boys,
and led him towards those so often inferior, all inferior
to himself, who had the naturalness along with the folly
of youth. Why should I try to explain? He went out
of the world, leaving a love - song or two behind him
and the little volume of " De Musset," of which much
was so well done, and yet some so badly done, and
nothing more to show for his life. And I to watch
it all going on day by day and year by year!

My Cecco took the first steps in the same way; but,
thanks be to God, righted himself and overcame—not

in time enough to save his career at Oxford, but so as
to be all that I had hoped,—always my very own, my
dearest companion, choosing me before all others. What
a companion he was, everybody who knew us knows:
full of knowledge, full of humour—a most accomplished
man, though to me always a boy. He did not make
friends easily, and he had few; but those whom he
had were very fond of him, and all our immediate surroundings looked up to him with an affectionate admiration which I cannot describe. " I don't know,
but I will ask Cecco," was what we all said. He had
not much more than emerged from the desert of temptation and trial, bringing balm and healing to me,
when he fell ill. When his illness first was declared,
it seemed to me that my misery was more than I
could bear. I remember that we all went to the Holy
Communion together the Sunday before we left for
Pau, and that as I went up to kneel at the altar I
was so nearly overcome, that Cyril put his hand on
my arm and gripped it almost roughly to recall me to
myself. And then the whole world seemed to come
back again into the sun after a time; he got so much
better, and the warm summer of the Queen's Jubilee
year seemed to complete what Pau had begun. And
he passed his examination for the British Museum,
coming out first, and his life seemed now to be ordered
in a safe place — in the work he loved. Alas! Then
Sir Andrew Clark would not pass him, but other
doctors gave the best of hopes. And he did a great
deal of good work, and finally went to the Royal Library
here; and we had many blinks of happiness, both in
the winter on the Riviera and at home. I cannot tell
what he was to me—consulting me about everything,
desiring to have me with him, to walk with me and
talk to me, only put out of humour when I was
drawn away or occupied by other things. When he
was absent he wrote to me every day. I never went

out but he was there to give me his arm. I seem to feel it now—the dear, thin, but firm arm. In the last four years after Cyril was taken from us, we were nearer and nearer. I can hear myself saying "Cecco and I." It was the constant phrase. But all through he was getting weaker: and I knew it, and tried not to know.

And now here I am all alone.

I cannot write any more.

LIST OF

MRS OLIPHANT'S PUBLISHED WORKS.

1870. John : A Love Story. 2 vols. . . . *Blackwood.*
" The Three Brothers. 3 vols. . . . *Hurst & Blackett.*
" Introductory Chapter to 'Life of Robert
     Lee,' by R. H. Story . . . .   "
1871. Squire Arden. 3 vols. . . . .   "
1872. At His Gates. 3 vols. . . . . *Tinsley.*
" Ombra, &c. 3 vols. . . . . . *Chapman & Hall.*
" Memoirs of the Count de Montalembert :
     A Chapter of recent French History . *Blackwood.*
1873. May. 3 vols. . . . . . . *Chapman & Hall.*
" Innocent : A Tale of Modern Life . . *Sampson Low.*
1874. A Rose in June. 2 vols. . . . . *Hurst & Blackett.*
" For Love and Life. 3 vols. . . .   "
1875. The Story of Valentine and his Brother.
     3 vols. . . . . *Blackwood.*
" Whiteladies. 3 vols. . . . . . *Chatto.*
" Preface to 'Art of Swimming in the Eton
     Style,' by J. Leahy . . . . *Macmillan.*
1876. The Curate in Charge. 2 vols. . . . *Beccles.*
" Phœbe, Junior : A Last Chronicle of Car-
     lingford. 3 vols. . . . . . *Hurst & Blackett.*
" Dress (*Art at Home Series*) . . . *Macmillan.*
" The Makers of Florence : Dante, Giotto,
     Savonarola, and their City . . .   "
1877. Foreign Classics for English Readers :
     Cervantes ; Dante ; and Molière (in
     conjunction with F. Tarver) . . . *Blackwood.*
" Young Musgrave. 3 vols. . . . . *Macmillan.*
" Mrs Arthur. 3 vols. . . . . . *Hurst & Blackett.*
" Carità. 3 vols. . . . . . . *Smith, Elder, & Co.*
1878. Postscript to 'Life of Anna Jameson,' by G.
     Macpherson . . . . . . *Longmans.*
" The Primrose Path : A Chapter in the
     Annals of the Kingdom of Fife. 3 vols. *Hurst & Blackett.*
1879. Within the Precincts. 3 vols. . . . *Smith, Elder, & Co.*
" The Two Mrs Scudamores (*Tales from
     Blackwood*) . . . . . . *Blackwood.*
" The Greatest Heiress in England. 3 vols. *Hurst & Blackett.*
1880. A Beleaguered City . . . . . *Macmillan.*
" He that Will Not when he May. 3 vols. .   "
1881. Harry Joscelyn. 3 vols. . . . . *Hurst & Blackett.*
1882. In Trust : A Story of a Lady and her Lover.
     3 vols. . . . . *Longmans.*
" Literary History of England in the End of
     the Eighteenth and Beginning of the
     Nineteenth Century. 3 vols. . . *Macmillan.*
" A Little Pilgrim in the Unseen . . .   "

1892. The Heir Presumptive and the Heir Ap-
       parent. 3 vols. .   .   .   .   . *Macmillan.*
1893. Lady William. 3 vols. .   .   .   .   "
  " The Sorceress. 3 vols. .   .   .   . *F. V. White.*
  " Thomas Chalmers, Preacher, Philosopher,
       and Statesman (*English Leaders of Re-*
       ligion) .   .   .   . *Methuen.*
1894. A House in Bloomsbury. 2 vols.   .   . *Hutchinson.*
  " Historical Sketches of the Reign of Queen
       Anne   .   .   .   . *Macmillan.*
  " Who was Lost and is Found   .   .   . *Blackwood.*
  " The Prodigals and their Inheritance. 2 vols. *Methuen.*
1895. A Child's History of Scotland   .   .   . *Fisher Unwin.*
  " Two Strangers .   .   .   .   .   .   "
  " Sir Robert's Fortune : A Story of a Scotch
       Moor   .   .   .   . *Methuen.*
  " The Makers of Modern Rome   .   .   . *Macmillan.*
1896. Jeanne d'Arc : Her Life and Death (*Heroes*
       of the Nations) .   .   .   .   . *Putnam.*
  " The Unjust Steward ; or, The Minister's
       Debt .   .   .   . *W. & R. Chambers.*
  " The Two Marys .   .   .   .   .   . *Methuen.*
  " Old Mr Tredgold   .   .   .   .   . *Longmans.*
1897. The Lady's Walk   .   .   .   .   . *Methuen.*
  " The Ways of Life. Two Stories   .   . *Smith, Elder, & Co.*
  " The Sisters Brontë (*Women Novelists*)   . *Hurst & Blackett.*
  " Annals of a Publishing House : William
       Blackwood and his Sons, their Magazine
       and Friends, vols. i., ii. .   .   .   . *Blackwood.*
1898. A Widow's Tale ; and other Stories .   .   "
  " That Little Cutty ; and Two other Stories . *Macmillan.*

MRS OLIPHANT'S CONTRIBUTIONS TO 'BLACKWOOD'S MAGAZINE.'

A Century of Great Poets—
 Walter Scott . . . . . . Aug. 1871.
 Wordsworth . . . . . . Sept. 1871.
American Books . . . . . . Oct. 1871.
New Books . . . .   "
A Century of Great Poets : Coleridge . . Nov. 1871.
The Two Mrs Scudamores . . . . Dec. 1871–Jan. 1872.
A Century of Great Poets : Burns . . . Feb. 1872.
Voltaire . . . . March 1872.
A Century of Great Poets : Shelley . . . April 1872.
New Books . . . . April and June 1872.
A Century of Great Poets : Byron . . . July 1872.
New Books . . . . Aug. 1872.
William Smith . . . . Oct. 1872.
A Century of Great Poets : Goethe . . . Dec. 1872.
New Books . . . . Dec. 1872 and Feb. 1873.
In London . . . . Feb. 1873.
Lord Lytton . . . . March 1873.
Kenelm Chillingley . . . . . . May 1873.
Alexandre Dumas . . . . . . July 1873.
A Century of Great Poets : Schiller . . Aug. 1873.
A Visit to Albion . . . . . .   "
New Books . . . . Sept. 1873.
A Railway Junction . . . . . . Oct. 1873.
New Books . . . . Nov. 1873.
The Story of Valentine . . . . . Jan. 1874–Feb. 1875.
The Indian Mutiny : Sir Hope Grant . . Jan. 1874.
Fables in Song . . . . Feb. 1874.
New Books . . . . April and June 1874.
Two Cities : Two Books . . . . . July 1874.
New Books . . . . Aug. 1874.
The Ancient Classics . . . . . Sept. 1874.
The Ancient Classics : Latin Literature . . Nov. 1874.
Life of the Prince Consort . . . . Jan. 1875.
New Books . . . . May 1875.
Art in May . . . . June 1875.
New Books . . . . July 1875.
Rivers . . . . Aug. 1875.
Michael Angelo . . . . . . Oct. 1875.
Lace and Bric-à-Brac . . . . . Jan. 1876.
A Century of Great Poets : Lamartine . . Feb. 1876.
Thackeray's Sketches . . . . .   "
Eton College . . . . March 1876.
Norman Macleod . . . . . . April 1876.
Macaulay . . . . May 1876.
The Royal Academy . . . . . June 1876.

Novels . . . . Dec. 1886.
The Land of Darkness . . . . . Jan. 1887.
The Old Saloon . . . . Jan., Feb., March, and April 1887.
Joyce . . . . May 1887–April 1888.
The Old Saloon . . . . . . May 1887.
The Rev. W. Lucas Collins . . . . "
The Old Saloon . . . . . . June 1887–Aug. 1887.
Marco Polo . . . . Sept. 1887.
The Old Saloon . . . . . Nov. 1887 and Jan. 1888.
Pictures of the Year . . . . . . June 1888.
The Old Saloon . . . . . . June and Sept. 1888.
On the Dark Mountains . . . . . Nov. 1888.
The Old Saloon . . . . . . Dec. 1888.
The Emperor Frederick . . . . . Jan. 1889.
Laurence Oliphant . . . . . . Feb. 1889.
The Old Saloon . . . . . . March and April 1889.
On the Riviera . . . . May 1889.
The Old Saloon . . June, Aug., Nov., Dec. 1889, and Jan. 1890.
Sons and Daughters . . . . . March and April 1890.
The Old Saloon . . . . . . March 1890.
Lord Lamington . . . . . . "
The Holy Land . . . . . . July 1890.
The Old Saloon . . . . . . Aug. and Nov. 1891.
Diana . . . . Feb. 1892–July 1892.
The Old Saloon . . . . . . Feb. 1892.
The Duke of Clarence . . . . . "
The City of St Andrews . . . . . March 1892.
The Old Saloon . . . . . . March and Oct. 1892.
Tennyson . . . . Nov. 1892.
The Old Saloon . . . . . . Dec. 1892.
A Visitor and his Opinions . . . . April 1893.
Marriage Bells . . . . . . July 1893.
Letters of Sir Walter Scott . . . . Jan. 1894.
Dean Stanley . . . . Feb. 1894.
Who was Lost and is Found . . . . June 1894–Nov. 1894.
The Looker-on . . . . Aug. 1894.
An Eton Master . . . . . . Nov. 1894.
The Looker-on . . . . Jan. 1895.
Fancies of a Believer . . . . . Feb. 1895.
Men and Women . . . . . . April 1895.
John Stuart Blackie . . . . . "
The Looker-on . . . . June and Dec. 1895.
Anti-Marriage League . . . . . Jan. 1896.
The Library Window . . . . . "
The Heirs of Kellie . . . . . . March 1896.
The Looker-on . . . . June and Oct. 1896.